LABORATORY Manual

MATHEMATICS

CBSE Class IX

LABORATORY Manual

MATHEMATICS

CBSE Class IX

Author

Hewanti Kushwaha, Priyanka Patel

Name..

Class......................... **Section**......................... **Roll No**........................

School..

Arihant Prakashan (School Division Series)

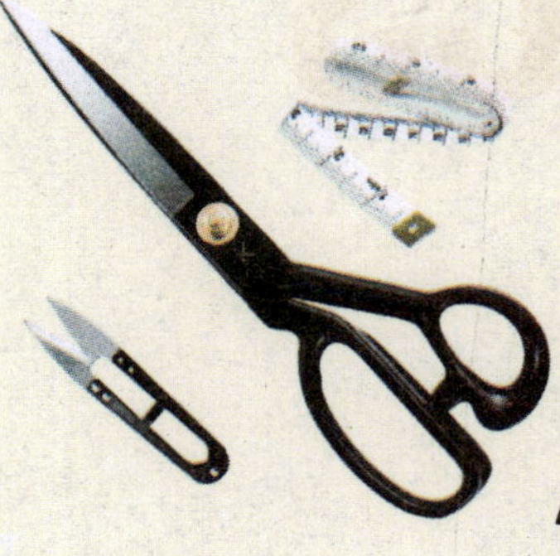

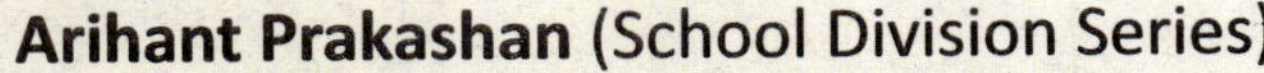

Arihant Prakashan (School Division Series)

All Rights Reserved

卐 © **Publishers**

No part of this publication may be re-produced, stored in a retrieval system or by any means, electronic mechanical, photocopying, recording, scanning, web or otherwise without the written permission of the publisher. Arihant has obtained all the information in this book from the sources believed to be reliable and true. However, Arihant or its editors or authors or illustrators don't take any responsibility for the absolute accuracy of any information published, and the damage or loss suffered there upon.

All disputes subject to Meerut (UP) jurisdiction only.

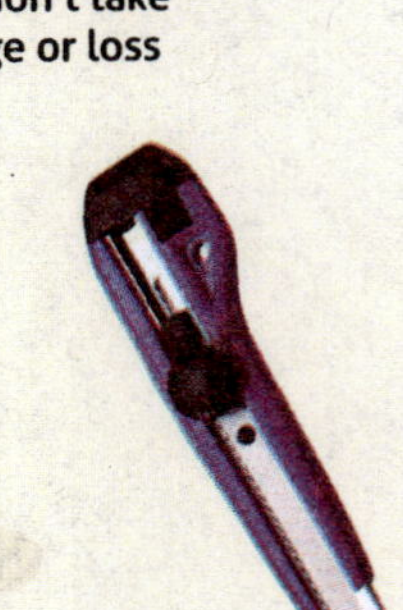

卐 **Administrative & Production Offices**

Regd. Office

'Ramchhaya' 4577/15, Agarwal Road, Darya Ganj, New Delhi -110002
Tele: 011- 47630600, 43518550; Fax: 011- 23280316

Head Office

Kalindi, TP Nagar, Meerut (UP) - 250002, Tele: 0121-7156203, 7156204

卐 **Sales & Support Offices**

Agra, Ahmedabad, Bengaluru, Bareilly, Chennai, Delhi, Guwahati, Hyderabad, Jaipur, Jhansi, Kolkata, Lucknow, Nagpur & Pune

卐 **Price :** ₹ 350.00

PO No. : TXT-29-T071422-6-26

Published by Arihant Publications (India) Ltd.

For further information about the books from Arihant,
log on to **www.arihantbooks.com** or email to **info@arihantbooks.com**

Follow us on   

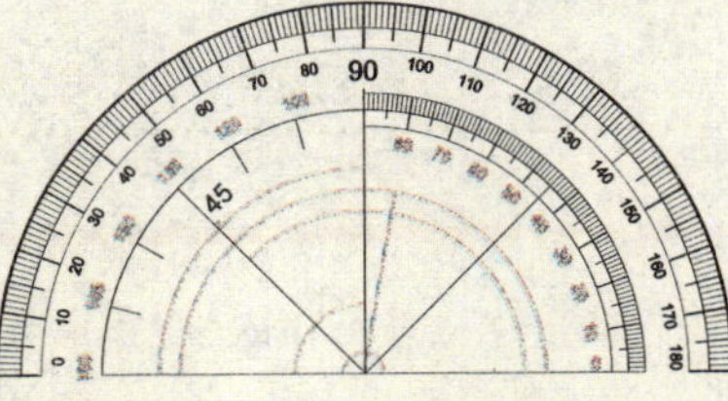

Contents

LIST OF ACTIVITIES

LIST OF PROJECTS

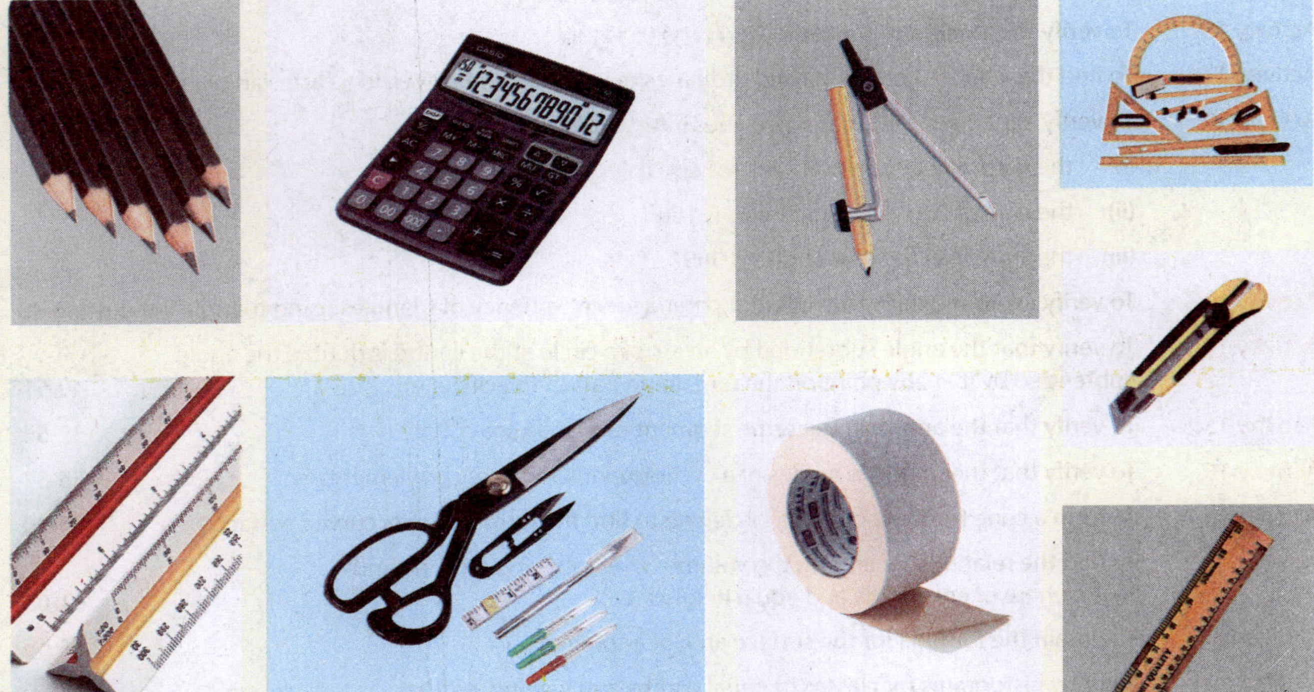

INDEX

S.No.	Name of the Activity/Project	Page No.	Date	Remarks

INDEX

S.No.	Name of the Activity/Project	Page No.	Date	Remarks

INDEX

S.No.	Name of the Activity/Project	Page No.	Date	Remarks

INDEX

S.No.	Name of the Activity/Project	Page No.	Date	Remarks

LABORATORY Manual

MATHEMATICS

CERTIFICATE

This is to certify that Activities &
Projects recorded in this Practical Notebook
have been performed by ______________________
(Student's name)

of __________ of ______________________________________
(class/section) (school name)

during academic session ______________________

.... Examiner Signature

.... Principal Signature (with school stamp)

.... Teacher Signature

The Purpose of The Mathematics Laboratory

The main objective of mathematics is to train the students to think and analysis the given situations and act logically. These objectives can only be achieved if there is an opportunity of creating a scope of exploring, verifying and experimenting upon mathematical results by students themselves.

Since, activities create interest among students who wants to explore and test some of their ideas, beliefs about mathematics and also present a problem or a challenge with the possibility of generating futher challenges and problems.

Mathematics laboratory is a place where scientific research and experiments are conducted for verification, exploration or discovery. The role of laboratory is helpful in understanding the mathematical concepts, formulae through activities.

A mathematics laboratory can foster mathematical awareness, skill building, positive attitude and learning by doing experiments in various topics of mathematics such as Algebra, Geometry, Mensuration, Coordinate Geometry, etc. It is the place where students can generate problem and struggle to a answer and learn certain concepts using concrete objects and verify many mathematical facts and properties using models, measurements and other activities.

The laboratory will act as a forum for the teachers to discuss and deliberate on some important mathematical issues and problems of the day.

Mathematics laboratory is expected to offer the following opportunities to learners:

- To discover the pattern for getting insight into the formulae.
- To visualise algebraic and analytical results geometrically.
- Offers more scope for individual participation. It encourages students to become independent learners.
- To encourage students in recognising, extending, formulating patterns and enabling them to pose problems in the form of conjectures.
- To exhibit relatedness of mathematics with day to day life problems.
- Builds up inherent interest and confidence in the students towards learning and doing mathematics.
- It helps to supplement the knowledge learned in classroom.

Role of Mathematics Laboratory in Teaching-Learning

The mathematics laboratory can contribute in a big way to the learning of this subject. Some of the ways are:

- Here, the student will get an opportunity to understand the abstract ideas/concepts through concrete objects and situations.
- The concepts of cylinder can be easily understood by making working models using rectangular or square paper.
- Height and distances concepts can only be conceived by trigonometric formulae in the laboratory, where as it is very difficult to understand these concepts on a black board.
- The concept of coordinate geometry, becomes very clear by drawing their graphs using mathematical instruments, which can be done in the laboratory.
- Since, the larger time available individually to the student and opportunity to repeat an activity several times, students can revise and rethink the problem and solutions. It helps to develop metacognitive abilities.
- It widens the experiential base and lays groundwork for later learning of new areas of mathematics and helps to make approprite connection between the known and unknown in mathematics.

Management and Maintenance of Laboratory

A laboratory is equipped with instruments, apparatus, equipments, models apart from facilities like water, electricity, etc. Non-availability of a single material or facility out of these may hinder the performance of any experiment activity in the laboratory. Therefore, the laboratory must be well managed and well maintained.

Personal Management and Maintenance

In personal management and maintenance following points are considered:

1. **Cleanliness** A laboratory should always be neat and clean. When students perform experiment activities during the day, it certainly becomes dirty and things are scattered. So, it is the duty of the lab staff to clean the laboratory.
2. **Checking and arranging materials for the day's work** Lab staff should know that what activities are going to be performed on a particular day. The material required for the day's activities must be arranged one day before.
3. The **facilities like water, electricity, etc.** must be checked and made available at the time of experiments.
4. Identify the **necessary materials** required in the laboratory by labeling them with name tags.
5. **Many safety measures** are required while working in laboratory. A list of such measures may be pasted on a wall of the laboratory.
6. Electrification of the laboratory should be professionally done to allow for safety use.
7. A **first aid kit** may be kept in the laboratory.

Management and Maintenance of Materials

To manage and maintain materials for a laboratory following points must be considered:

1. A list of instruments, apparatus, activities and material may be prepared according to the experiments included in the syllabus of mathematics.
2. Arrange the materials in places (on tables, shelves, board, etc) in a way that they can be easily accessed when needed and returned appropriately after use.
3. The instruments, equipments and apparatus should also be checked regularly by the laboratory staff. If any repair is required it should be done immediately.
4. Arrange the benches and tables to allow for free movement in the laboratory.

Materials and Equipments for Mathematics Laboratory

As the students will be involved in a lot of model making activities under the guidance of the teacher, the smooth running of the mathematics laboratory will depend upon the supply of oddments such as strings and threads, cellotape, white cardboard, hardboard, needles and pins, drawing pins, sandpaper, pliers, screwdrivers, rubber bands of different colours, gummed papers and labels, squared papers, plywood, scissors, saw, paint, soldering, solder wire, steel wire, cotton wool, tin and plastic sheets, glazed papers, overhead projector, slide projector etc.

Besides these, some models, charts, slides, etc. made up of a good durable material should also be there for the teacher to demonstrate some mathematical concepts, facts and properties before the students.

Different tables, ready reckner should also be there (in the laminated form) so that these can be used by the students for different purposes.

In view of the above, following is the list of suggested instruments/models for the laboratory:

Equipment

Mathematical instrument set (Wooden Geometry Box for demonstration containing rulers, set-squares, divider, protractor and compasses), some geometry boxes, metre scales of 100 cm, 50 cm and 30 cm, measuring tape, diagonal scale, clinometer, calculators, computers including related software etc.

Models

For demonstration of

- Number System
- Algebra
- Coordinate geometry
- Geometry
- Mensuration
- Statistics
- Probability

Activities

Activity 1

OBJECTIVE

To construct a square root spiral.

Prior Knowledge

1. Concept of number line
2. Concept of irrational numbers
3. Pythagoras theorem

Materials Required

1. Adhesive/fevicol/gum etc.
2. Geometry box
3. Coloured pens
4. A drawing sheet

Theory

1. A **number line** is a line whose each point represents a real number.
2. Irrational numbers are those numbers which cannot be expressed in the form $\frac{p}{q}$, where $q \neq 0$ and both p and q are integers. e.g. $\sqrt{3}$, π, etc.
3. Pythagoras theorem state that in a right angled triangle, the square of the hypotenuse is equal to the sum of the squares of other two sides containing right angle. ΔPQR is a right angled triangle and $\angle Q = 90°$. (see Fig. 1.1)

   Therefore, $(PR)^2 = (PQ)^2 + (QR)^2$

   where, PR = hypotenuse, PQ = perpendicular and QR = base

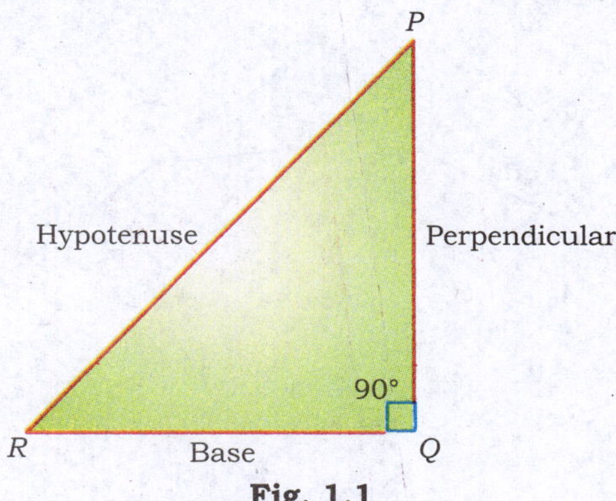

Fig. 1.1

Procedure

1. Take a drawing sheet of any size and mark a point L on it.
2. Draw a line segment L of length 1 unit by taking 2 cm as 1 unit. (see Fig. 1.2)

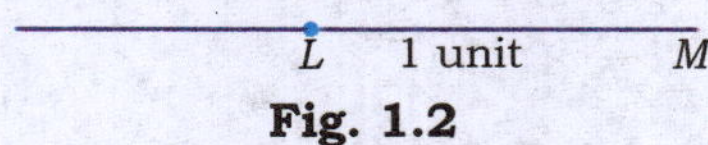

Fig. 1.2

3. Construct a line MX perpendicular to the line segment LM, by using a pair of compasses or a set square. (see Fig. 1.3)

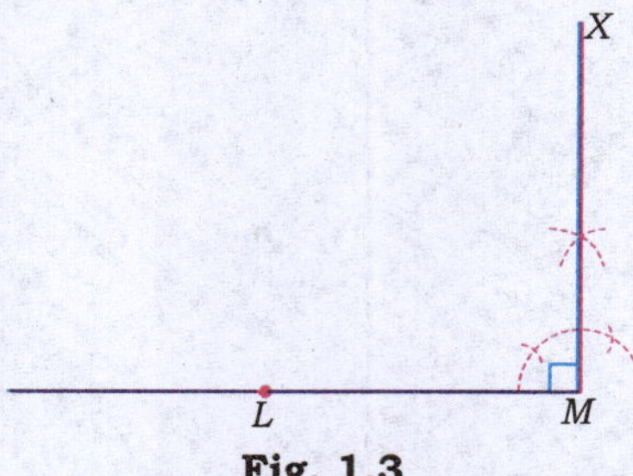

Fig. 1.3

4. From M, draw an arc of 1 unit (= 2 cm) which cut MX at N(say). (see Fig. 1.4)

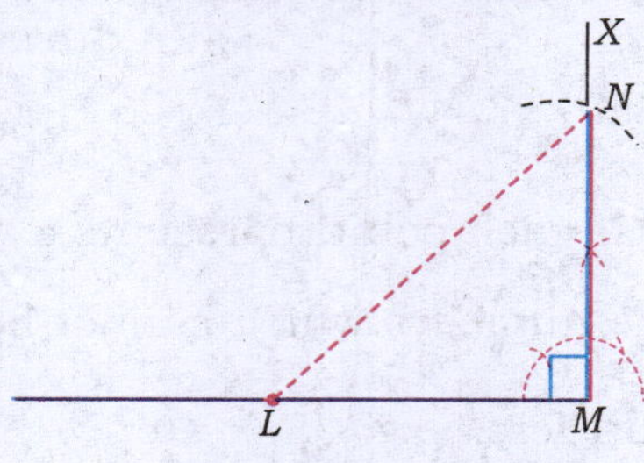

Fig. 1.4

5. Join LN through a dotted line.
6. Taking LN as base, draw a perpendicular NY to LN, by using a pair of compasses or a set square.
7. From N, draw an arc of 1 unit (x m), which cut NY at O (say).
8. Join LO through a dotted line.

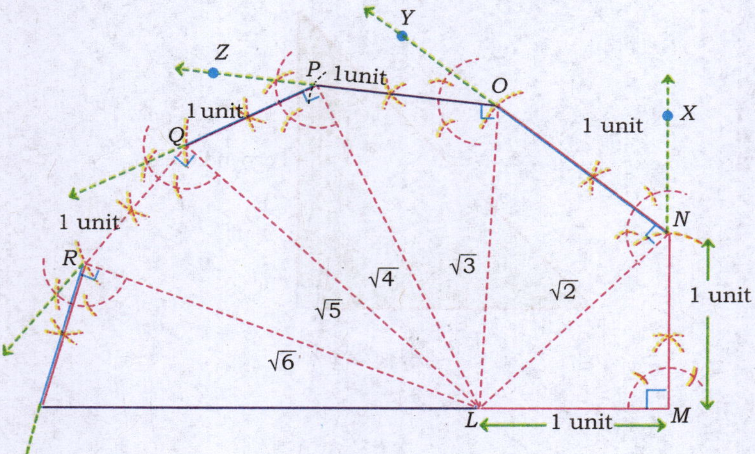

Fig. 1.5

9. Keep repeating the above process for sufficient number of times to get the 'square root spiral' as shown in Fig 1.5.

Observations

In the Fig. 1.5, ΔLMN is a right angled triangle right angle at M.

$\therefore$ By Pythagoras theorem, we have

$$(LN)^2 = (LM)^2 + (MN)^2 \quad [\because (\text{Hypotenuse})^2 = (\text{Perpendicular})^2 + (\text{Base})^2]$$

$$= 1^2 + 1^2 = 2$$

$\Rightarrow$ $LN = \sqrt{2}$ [taking positive square root]

Again, ΔLNO is also a right angled triangle right angle at N.

$\therefore$ By Pythagoras theorem,

$$(LO)^2 = (LN)^2 + (NO)^2$$

$$= (\sqrt{2})^2 + (1)^2 = 2 + 1 = 3$$

$\Rightarrow$ $L = \sqrt{3}$ [taking positive square root]

Similarly, we have

$L = \sqrt{4}$

$\Rightarrow$ $L = \sqrt{5}$

$\Rightarrow$ $L = \sqrt{6}$ and so on.

By actual measurement, we get

$LN =$ .... , $LO =$ .... , $LP =$ .... ,

$LQ =$ .... , $LR =$ ....

Thus,

$\sqrt{2} = LN =$ .... (approx.) $\sqrt{3} = LO =$ .... (approx.)

$\sqrt{4} = LP =$ .... (approx.) $\sqrt{5} = LQ =$ .... (approx.)

$\sqrt{6} = LR =$ .... (approx.)

Result

A square root spiral has been constructed.

Application

Existence of irrational numbers can be illustrated with the help of this activity.

Viva-Voce

Q.1 Define a rational number.

Ans A number which can be expressed in the form of $\frac{p}{q}$, where $q \neq 0$ and p, q are integers, is called a rational number.

Q.2 Define an irrational number.

Ans A number which cannot be expressed in the form of $\frac{p}{q}$, where $q \neq 0$ and p, q are integers, is called an irrational number.

Q.3 Define a real number.

Ans A number which may be either rational or irrational, is called a real number.

Q.4 How many rational and irrational numbers lie between any two real numbers?

Ans There are infinite rational and irrational numbers lie between any two real numbers.

Q.5 Is it possible to represent irrational numbers on the number line?

Ans Yes, as we know that each point on the number line represent a real number (i.e. both rational and irrational), so irrational number can be represented on number line.

Q.6 Which theorem have you used for finding the hypotenuse of right angled triangle.

Ans Pythagoras theorem.

Q.7 If n is a natural number, then what is $\sqrt{n}$?

Ans Either natural number or irrational number.

Q.8 Is it true that decimal expansion of a rational number, either terminating or non-terminating.

Ans Yes

Q.9 In a square root spiral, is it true that square root of each of natural numbers (> 1), is equal to the square root of the sum of 1 and previous natural number (> 1) ?

Ans Yes

Q.10 Is it possible that we make a square root spiral of negative numbers?

Ans No

Activity 2

OBJECTIVE

To represent some irrational numbers on the number line.

Prior Knowledge

1. Concept of number line.
2. Concept of irrational numbers.
3. Pythagoras theorem.

Materials Required

1. Two cuboidal wooden strips
2. Thread
3. Nails
4. Hammer
5. Two paper scales
6. A screw with nut
7. Glue
8. Cutter

Theory

1. For concept of number line refer to Activity 1.
2. For concept of irrational numbers refer to Activity 1.
3. For Pythagoras theorem refer to Activity 1.

Procedure

1. Make a straight slit on the top of one of the the wooden strips. Now, fix another wooden strip on the slit perpendicular to the former strip with a screw at the bottom, so that it can move freely along the slit. (see Fig. 2.1)

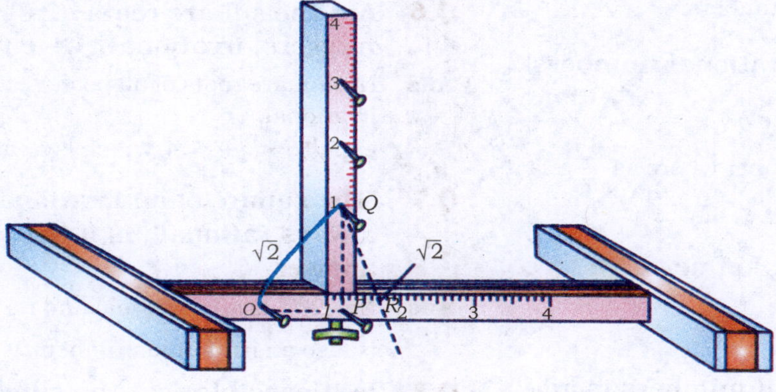

Fig. 2.1

2. Paste one paper scale on the horizontal strip and another paper scale on the perpendicular (i.e. vertical) strip. (see Fig. 2.1)
3. Fix nails at a distance of 1 unit each, starting from 0, on both the strips. (see Fig. 2.1)
4. Now, tie a thread at the nail at point O representing 0 on the horizontal strip. (see Fig. 2.1)
5. With the help of screw, fix the perpendicular wooden strip at point 'P' representing 1 unit on horizontal scale.
6. Tie the other end of the thread at point *Q* representing 1 unit on the perpendicular strip.

7. Remove the thread from unit 1 on the perpendicular strip and place it on the horizontal strip to represent $\sqrt{2}$ on the number line. Thus, OR represents $\sqrt{2}$ on the number line.
8. Similarly, to represent $\sqrt{3}$, fix the perpendicular wooden strip at $\sqrt{2}$ and repeat the above process.

Observation

ΔOPQ is a right angled triangle right angle at P.

By Pythagoras theorem, $(OQ)^2 = (OP)^2 + (PQ)^2$, [Here, $OP = 1$ unit, $PQ = 1$ unit,]

$\therefore \quad (OQ)^2 = (1)^2 + (1)^2$

$\Rightarrow \quad OQ^2 = 2 \Rightarrow OQ = \sqrt{2}$ [taking positive square root]

$\therefore \quad (OR)^2 = (OQ)^2 = (\sqrt{2})^2$

Note *To find $\sqrt{a}$ such as $\sqrt{13}$, fix the perpendicular strip at 3 on the horizontal strip and tie the other end of thread at 2 on the vertical strip.*

Result

Any irrational number can be represented on the number line by using this method.

Application

This activity may help to student in representing some irrational numbers like $\sqrt{2}, \sqrt{3}, \sqrt{5}, \sqrt{6}, \sqrt{7}, \ldots$, etc., on the number line.

Viva-Voce

Q.1 Is every irrational number, a real number? Justify your answer.

Ans Yes, because real numbers consist of both rational and irrational numbers.

Q.2 'π and $\frac{22}{7}$ are both irrational numbers'. Is this statement true?

Ans No, π is an irrational number where as $\frac{22}{7}$ is a rational number.

Q.3 What is the reciprocal of negative irrational number?

Ans Irrational number.

Q.4 'Sum of two irrational numbers is an irrational number'. Is this statement true?

Ans No, its not true, sum of two irrational numbers may be irrational or rational.

Q.5 Is the product of two irrational numbers, an irrational number? Give reasons.

Ans No, it is not necessary that, the product of two irrational numbers is irrational number. e.g. product of $\sqrt{20}$ and $\sqrt{5}$ is 10, a rational number.

Q.6 Are the square roots of all positive integers, irrational? Give reason.

Ans No, square roots of all positive integers do not irrational. e.g. $\sqrt{16} = \sqrt{4^2} = 4$, which is a rational number.

Q.7 'The square of an irrational number is always rational'. Is it true? Justify your answer.

Ans No, $(2)^{1/4}$ is an irrational and its square $(2^{1/4})^2 = 2^{1/2}$ is also an irrational number.

Q.8 Is it possible that the sum of two irrational numbers can be represented on number line?

Ans Yes

Q.9 Can we apply Pythagoras theorem in any triangle?

Ans No, Pythagoras theorem is applicable only in right angled triangle.

Activity 3

OBJECTIVE

To verify the algebraic identity $(x + y)^2 = x^2 + 2xy + y^2$

Prior Knowledge

1. Rectangle and its area
2. Square and its area

Materials Required

1. Drawing sheet
2. Pencil
3. Cello-tape
4. Coloured papers
5. Cutter
6. Ruler

Theory

1. A **rectangle** is a parallelogram whose opposite sides are equal and each angle is equal to 90°. (see fig. 3.1)

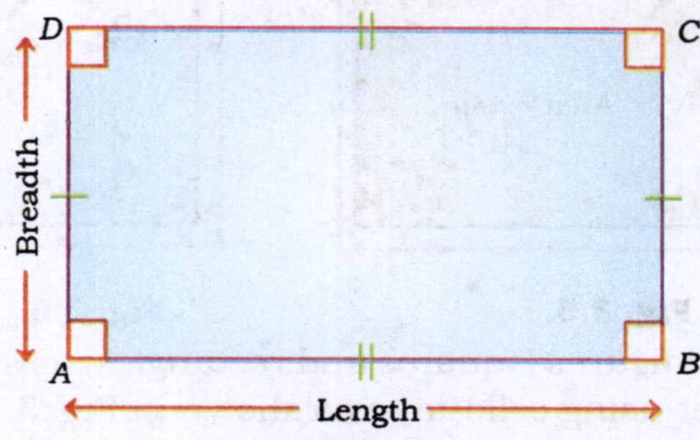

Fig. 3.1

Area of rectangle = Length × Breadth

2. A **square** is a rectangle whose all sides are equal. (see fig. 3.2)

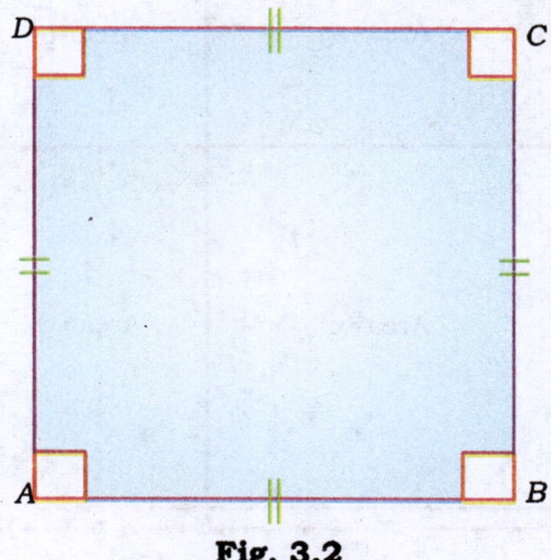

Fig. 3.2

Area of square = $(\text{Side})^2$

Procedure

1. From a coloured paper, cut out a square whose length of each side is x units (say $x = 5$ cm) and name it as square *DEFG*. (see Fig. 3.3)
2. From the same coloured paper as in step 1st, cut out another square whose length of each side is y units ($y < x$ say $y = 3$ cm) and name it as square *FIJK*. (see Fig 3.4)

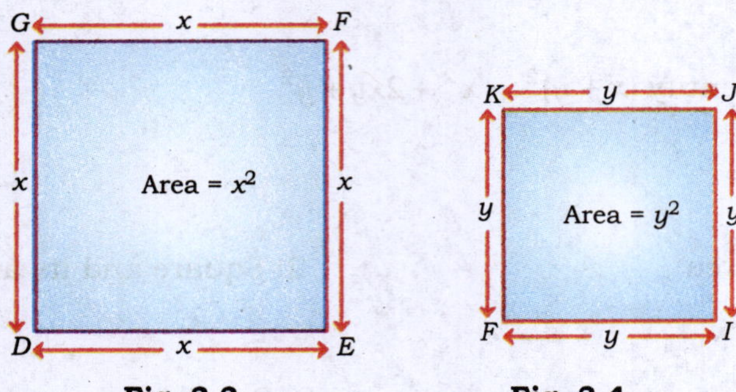

Fig. 3.3 Fig. 3.4

3. From different coloured paper, cut out two rectangles of length x and y units and breadth y and x units, respectively and name them as rectangle *GFKO* and *EQIF*, respectively. (see Fig. 3.5 and Fig. 3.6)

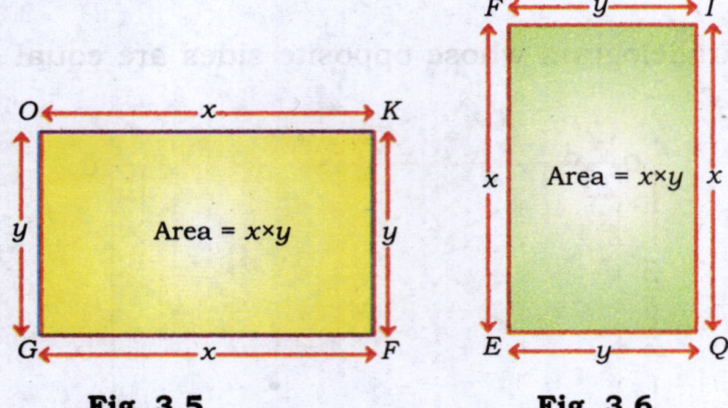

Fig. 3.5 Fig. 3.6

4. Arrange the above cutted figures (squares and rectangles) as shown in the above figure and paste it on drawing sheet using cello-tape as shown in Fig. 3.7. From figure 3.7, it is clear that we have obtained a square *DQJO* of side $(x + y)$.

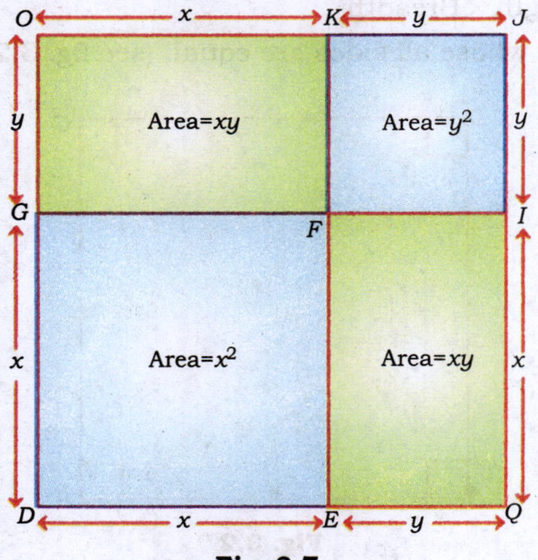

Fig. 3.7

Observation

From Fig. 3.7, area of *DQJO*

$= \text{Area of square } DEFG + \text{Area of rectangle } EQIF$

$+ \text{Area of square } FIJK + \text{Area of rectangle } GFKO$

$= (x^2 + xy + y^2 + xy) \text{ sq units} = (x^2 + y^2 + 2xy) \text{ sq units}$

Also, *DQJO* is a square of side $(x + y)$.

So, area of $DQJO = (x + y)^2$ sq units ...(ii)

Hence, from Eqs. (i) and (ii), we have

$$(x + y)^2 = x^2 + 2xy + y^2$$

On actual measurement, we get

$x =$ ...., $y =$ ...., $(x + y) =$ ....

Now, $x^2 =$ ...., $y^2 =$ ...., $xy =$ ....,

$(x + y)^2 =$ ...., $2xy =$ ....

Hence, $(x + y)^2 = x^2 + 2xy + y^2$.

The identity may be verified by taking different values of x and y.

Result

The identity $(x + y)^2 = x^2 + 2xy + y^2$ has been verified.

Applications

The identity is useful for

1. calculating the square of a number, which can be expressed as the sum of the two convenient numbers.
2. simplification and factorisation of some algebraic expressions.

Viva-Voce

Q.1 What do you mean by algebraic expression?

Ans A combination of constants and variables, connected by four fundamental arithmetic operations $+, -, \times$ and $\div$ is called an algebraic expression.

Q.2 Are $(a + b)^2$ and $a^2 + 2ab + b^2$ algebraic expressions?

Ans Yes, both $(a + b)^2$ and $a^2 + 2ab + b^2$ are algebraic expressions because they contain both variables (a and b) and arithmetic operations $(+, \times)$.

Q.3 What is the difference between algebraic expression and polynomial?

Ans In algebraic expression, variables may have negative exponents but in polynomial, variables have only positive integer powers.

Q.4 Is $a^2 + 2ab + b^2$ a polynomial? Give reasons.

Ans Yes, because the variables a and b have positive integer powers.

Q.5 On the basis of degree, name the type of polynomial '$a^2 + 2ab + b^2$'.

Ans Quadratic polynomial

Q.6 What is the degree of zero polynomial?

Ans Not defined.

Activity 4

OBJECTIVE

To verify the algebraic identity $(x-y)^2 = x^2 - 2xy + y^2$

Prior Knowledge

1. Rectangle and its area.
2. Square and its area.

Materials Required

1. Drawing sheet
2. Pencil
3. Coloured papers
4. A pair scissors
5. Geometry box
6. Adhesive

Theory

1. For rectangle and its area refer to Activity 3.
2. For square and its area refer to Activity 3.

Procedure

1. From a coloured paper, cut out a square *ABCD* of side x units (say. $x = 5$ cm). (see Fig. 4.1)
2. Further, cut out another square *EBFG* of side y units such that $y < x$ (say $y = 3$ cm) (see Fig. 4.2)

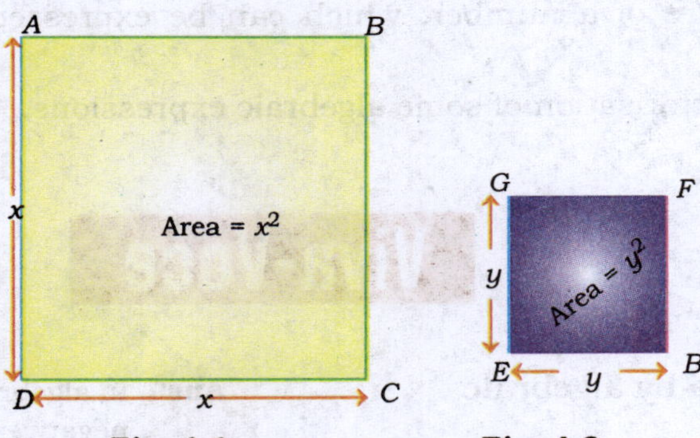

Fig. 4.1 **Fig. 4.2**

3. Now, cut out a rectangle *DCIH* of length x units and breadth y units from another coloured paper. (see Fig. 4.3)

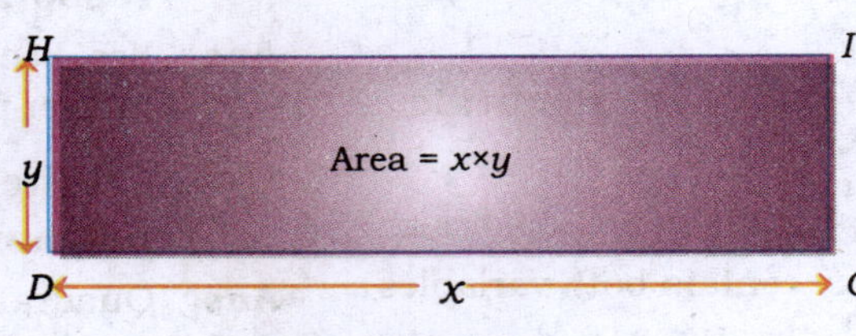

Fig. 4.3

4. Now further, cut out another rectangle *KIFG* of length *y* units and breadth *x* units. (see Fig. 4.4)

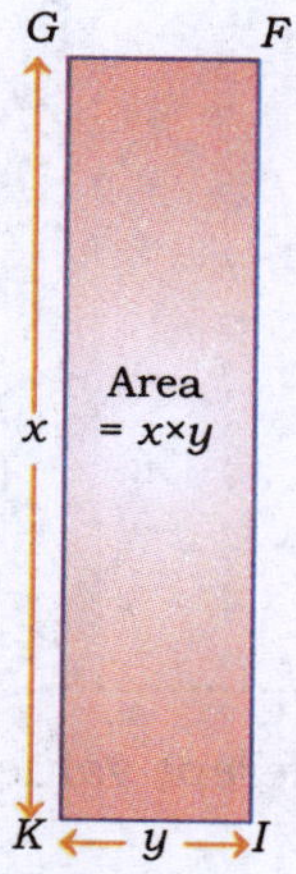

Fig. 4.4

5. Now, arrange figures 4.1, 4.2, 4.3 and 4.4, according to their vertices and paste it on a drawing sheet. (see Fig. 4.5)

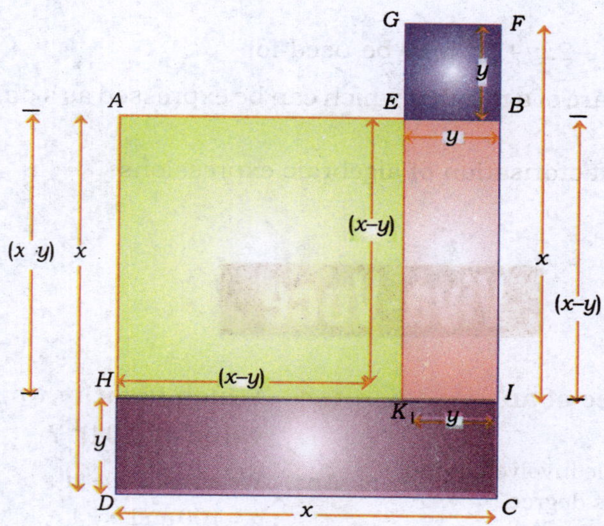

Fig. 4.5

Observation

From the figures 4.1, 4.2, 4.3 and 4.4, we have

Area of square $ABCD = x^2$ sq unit

Area of square $EBFG = y^2$ sq unit

Area of rectangle $DCIH = xy$ sq unit

and Area of rectangle $KIFG = xy$ sq unit

Area of square $AHKE$ = Area of square $ABCD$ + Area of square $EBFG$ – Area of rectangle $KIFG$ – Area of rectangle $DCIH$

$$= x^2 + y^2 - xy - xy$$

$$= x^2 - 2xy + y^2 \qquad \ldots(i)$$

Also, from Fig. 4.5, it is clear that $AHKE$ is a square whose each side is $(x-y)$.

Area of square $AHKE = (\text{Side})^2 = [(x-y)]^2 = (x-y)^2$ sq unit ...(ii)

From Eqs. (i) and (ii), we get

$$(x-y)^2 = x^2 - 2xy + y^2$$

Here, area is in square units.

On actual measurement, we get

$x = \ldots\ldots$, $y = \ldots\ldots$, $(x-y) = \ldots\ldots$,

So, $x^2 = \ldots\ldots$, $y^2 = \ldots\ldots$, $(x-y)^2 = \ldots\ldots$, $xy = \ldots\ldots\ldots\ldots$

and $2xy = \ldots\ldots$.

Hence, $(x-y)^2 = x^2 - 2xy + y^2 = \ldots\ldots\ldots\ldots\ldots\ldots$

The identity may be verified by taking different values of x and y.

Result

Algebraic identity $(x-y)^2 = x^2 - 2xy + y^2$ has been verified.

Applications

The identity $(x-y)^2 = x^2 - 2xy + y^2$ may be used for

1. calculating the square of a number which can be expressed as a difference of two convenient numbers.
2. simplification and factorisation of algebraic expressions.

Viva-Voce

Q.1 What do we mean by degree of an algebraic expression?

Ans The highest power of the variable involved in the algebraic expression is called its degree.

Q.2 What do you mean by an algebraic identity?

Ans An algebraic identity is an algebraic equation which is true for all values of variables occurring in it.

Q.3 Is $(x-3y)^2 = x^2 - 6xy + 9y^2$ an algebraic identity?

Ans Yes

Q.4 Is the identity $(a-b)^2 = a^2 - 2ab + b^2$ hold for negative values of a and b?

Ans Yes

Q.5 Can you find the value of 99^2 using the identity $(a-b)^2 = a^2 - 2ab + b^2$?

Ans Yes

Q.6 Which identity would you use to find the value of $(101)^2$?

Ans We should use $(a+b)^2 = a^2 + 2ab + b^2$ by taking $a = 100$ and $b = 1$

Q.7 Suppose we want square of any natural number, then it is possible to find the square of any natural number by using the identity $(a-b)^2 = a^2 + b^2 - 2ab$

Ans Yes

Q.8 In the identity $(a-b)^2 = a^2 + b^2 - 2ab$, if both variables are equal, then what is the the value of $(a-b)^2$?

Ans When $a = b$, then $(a-b)^2 = (b-b)^2 = 0$

Q.9 The algebric identity is true for every real number.

Ans Yes

Activity 5

OBJECTIVE

To verify the algebraic identity $x^2 - y^2 = (x + y)(x - y)$.

Prior Knowledge

1. Rectangle and its area.
2. Square and its area.
3. Trapezium.

Materials Required

1. Drawing sheet
2. Pencil
3. Coloured papers
4. A pair of Scissors
5. Sketch pen
6. Geometry box
7. Adhesive

Theory

1. For rectangle and its area refer to Activity 3.
2. For square and its area refer to Activity 3.
3. **Trapezium** is a quadrilateral whose one pair of opposite sides are parallel and other pair of opposite sides are non-parallel.

   In the trapezium *PQRS*, (see fig. 5.1) sides *PQ* and *SR* are parallel while sides *PS* and *QR* are non-parallel.

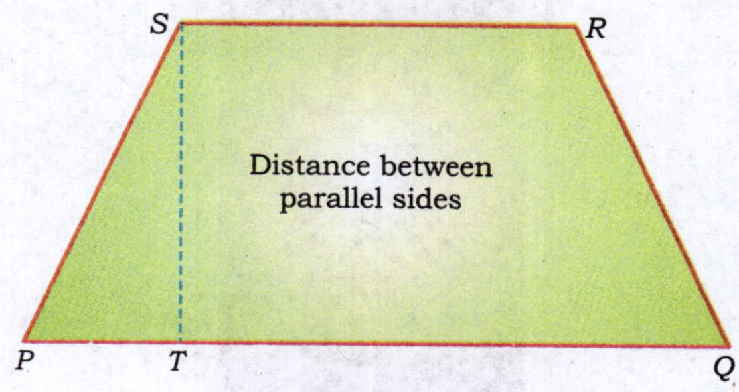

Fig. 5.1

Area of trapezium $= \frac{1}{2} \times$ Sum of parallel sides $\times$ Distance between parallel sides

$$= \frac{1}{2}(PQ + RS) \times ST$$

Procedure

1. Cut out a square *ABCD* of side x units (say $x = 7$ cm) from a coloured paper. (see Fig. 5.2)
2. Cut out a square *DEFG* of side y units (say $y = 5$ cm) $(y < x)$ from another coloured paper. (see Fig. 5.3)
3. Paste the smaller square *DEFG* on the bigger square *ABCD* as shown in Fig. 5.4.

4. Join the points F and B using sketch pen. (see Fig. 5.4)

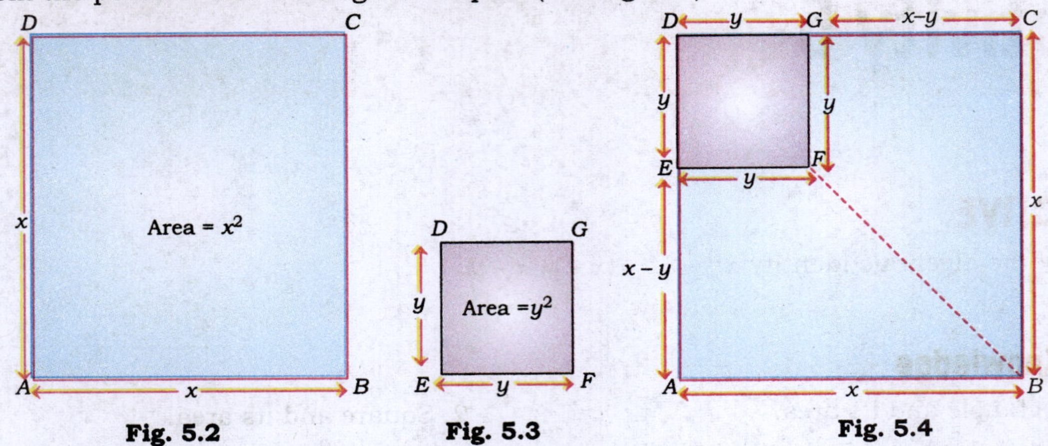

Fig. 5.2 Fig. 5.3 Fig. 5.4

5. Cut out the trapeziums $GFBC$ and $ABFE$ from square $ABCD$ (see Fig. 5.5 and 5.6).

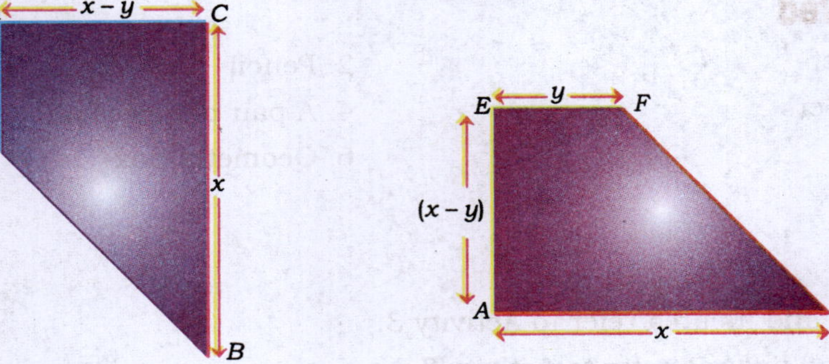

Fig. 5.5 Fig. 5.6

6. Paste both trapeziums obtained in step 5 on the drawing sheet as shown in Fig. 5.7

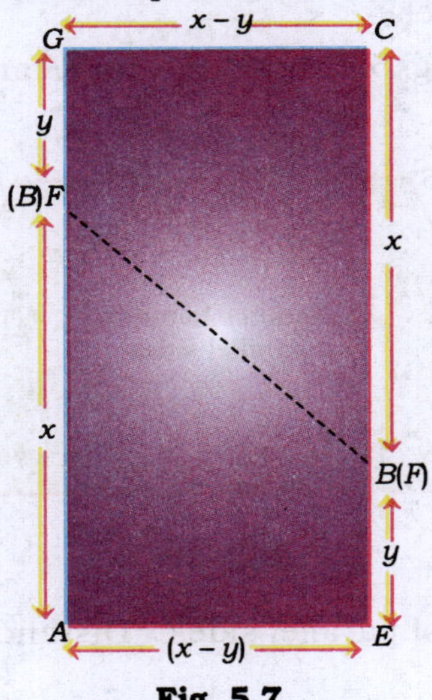

Fig. 5.7

Observation

From Fig. 5.2 and Fig. 5.3, we have

Area of square $ABCD = x^2$ sq unit

Area of square $DEFG = y^2$ sq unit

Now, from Fig. 5.4, we have

Area of square $ABCD$ – Area of square $DEFG$

= Area of trapezium $GFBC$ + Area of trapezium $ABFE$

= Area of rectangle $AECG$ [from Fig. 5.7]

= $AG \cdot AE$ [$\because$ Area of rectangle = Length $\times$ Breadth]

So, $x^2 - y^2 = (x+y)(x-y)$ [$\because AG = x + y,\ AE = x - y$]

Here, area is in square units.

On actual measurement, we get

$x = \ldots\ldots,\quad y = \ldots\ldots$

So, $y^2 = \ldots\ldots,\quad x^2 = \ldots\ldots,$

$x + y = \ldots\ldots,\quad x - y = \ldots\ldots,$

$x^2 - y^2 = \ldots\ldots$ and $(x+y)(x-y) = \ldots\ldots$

Hence, $x^2 - y^2 = (x+y)(x-y)$

The identity may be verified by taking different values of a and b.

Result

The algebraic identity $x^2 - y^2 = (x+y)(x-y)$ has been verified.

Applications

The identity $x^2 - y^2 = (x+y)(x-y)$ can be used for

1. calculating the difference of squares of two numbers.
2. getting some products involving two numbers.
3. simplification and factorisation of algebraic expressions.

Viva-Voce

Q.1 Which algebraic identity should be used to evaluate $(65)^2 - (35)^2$?

Ans $a^2 - b^2 = (a+b)(a-b)$

Q.2 If the sides of a rectangle are $(\sqrt{3}+\sqrt{2})$ units and $(\sqrt{3}-\sqrt{2})$ units, then what will be its area?

Ans $(\sqrt{3}+\sqrt{2})(\sqrt{3}-\sqrt{2}) = (\sqrt{3})^2 - (\sqrt{2})^2 = 3 - 2 = 1$ sq unit

Q.3 Is $a^2 - b^2$ a monomial? Justify.

Ans No, $a^2 - b^2$ is a binomial because it has two terms.

Q.4 What is the degree of identity $a^2 - b^2 = (a-b)(a+b)$.

Ans The degree of given identity is two.

Q.5 What is the degree of trinomial?

Ans Any number, as degree depends on exponent of a variable.

Q.6 How many terms are there in quadratic polynomial in one variable?

Ans Maximum three.

Q.7 Is the algebraic identity $a^2 - b^2 = (a-b)(a+b)$, true for only natural numbers?

Ans No, it is true for all real numbers.

Q.8 If we take both negative variables, then is their any change in algebraic identity $a^2 - b^2 = (a+b)(a-b)$. Justify your answer.

Ans No,

We know, $a^2 - b^2 = (a+b)(a-b)$

Suppose we take $a = -a$ and $b = -b$,

then $(-a)^2 - (-b)^2 = (-a-b)(-a+b)$

$\Rightarrow a^2 - b^2 = (a-b)(a+b)$

Q.9 Is the algebraic identity $a^2 - b^2 = (a+b)(a-b)$ also true, if any one of the variable in the given identity is zero? Justify.

Ans Yes, suppose $b = 0$, then

$a^2 - 0^2 = (a+0)(a-0) \Rightarrow a^2 = a^2$, true.

Activity 6

OBJECTIVE

To verify the algebraic identity $(x+y+z)^2 = x^2 + y^2 + z^2 + 2xy + 2yz + 2zx$.

Prior Knowledge

1. Rectangle and its area.
2. Square and its area.

Materials Required

1. Hardboard
2. Coloured papers
3. Adhesive
4. White paper
5. A pair of scissors
6. Geometry Box

Theory

1. For rectangle and its area refer to Activity 3.
2. For square and its area refer to Activity 3.

Procedure

1. Take a hardboard of suitable size and paste a white paper on it.
2. From a coloured paper, cut out a square of side x units (say $x = 8$ cm). (see Fig. 6.1)
3. Further, cut out a square of side y units say $y = 6$ cm $(y < x)$ from another coloured paper. (see Fig. 6.2)
4. Also, cut out a square of side z units say $z = 4$ cm $(z < y)$ from same coloured paper as in step 2. (see Fig. 6.3)

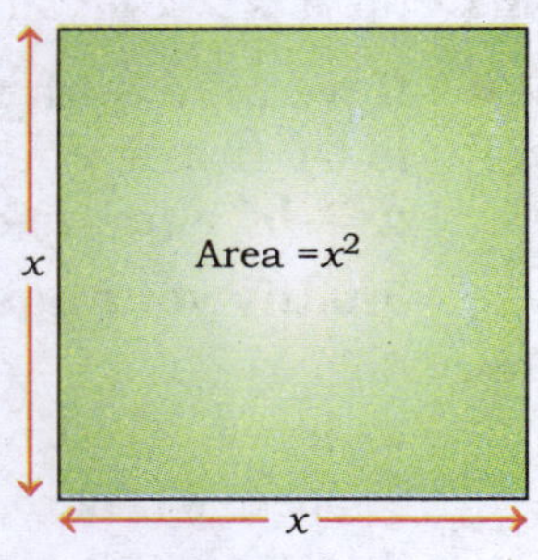

Fig. 6.1

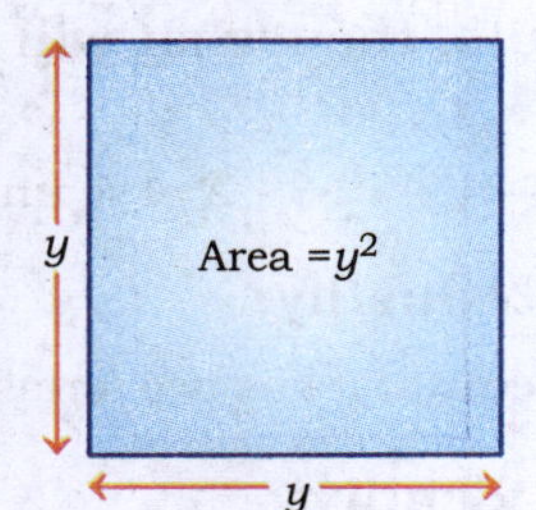

Fig. 6.2

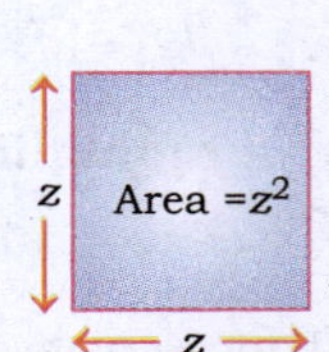

Fig. 6.3

5. Cut out two rectangles of dimensions $x \times y$ from same coloured paper as in step 3. (see Fig. 6.4)

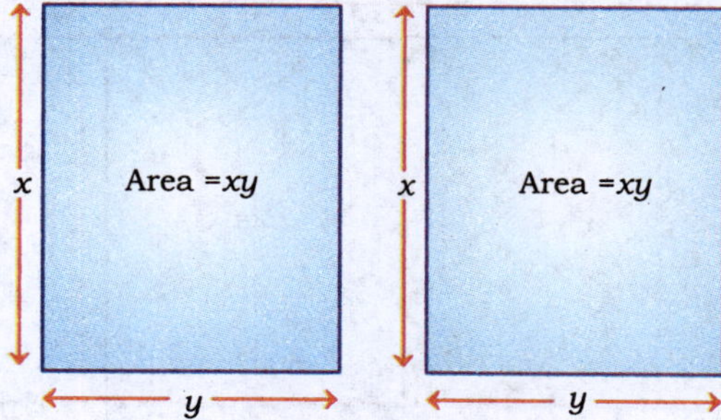

Fig. 6.4

6. Also, cut out two rectangles of dimensions $y \times z$ from same coloured paper as in step 2. (see Fig. 6.5)

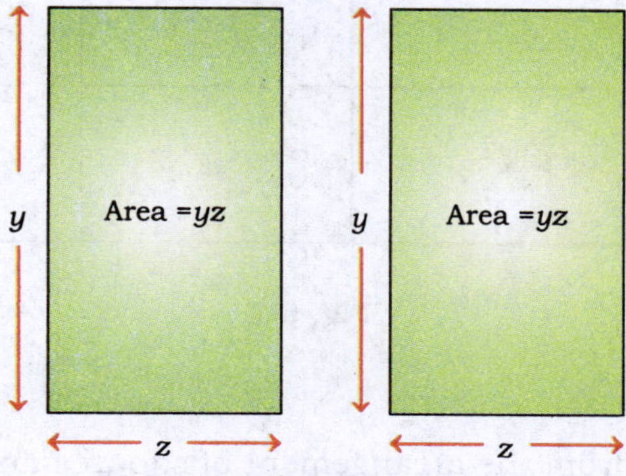

Fig. 6.5

7. Now further, cut out two rectangles of dimensions $x \times z$ from same coloured paper as in step 3. (see Fig. 6.6)

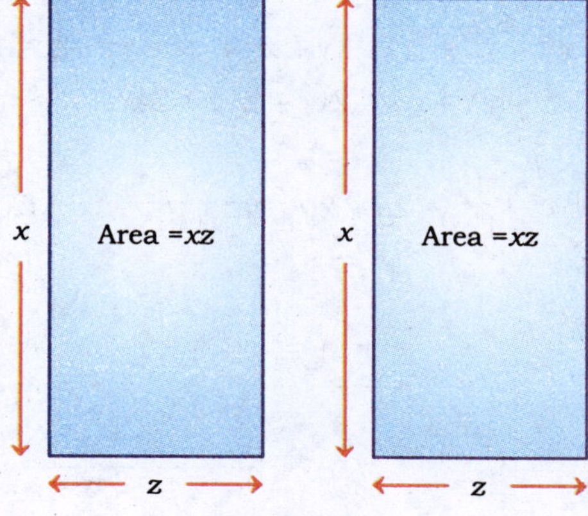

Fig. 6.6

8. Paste the squares and rectangles on the hardboard as shown in Fig. 6.7.

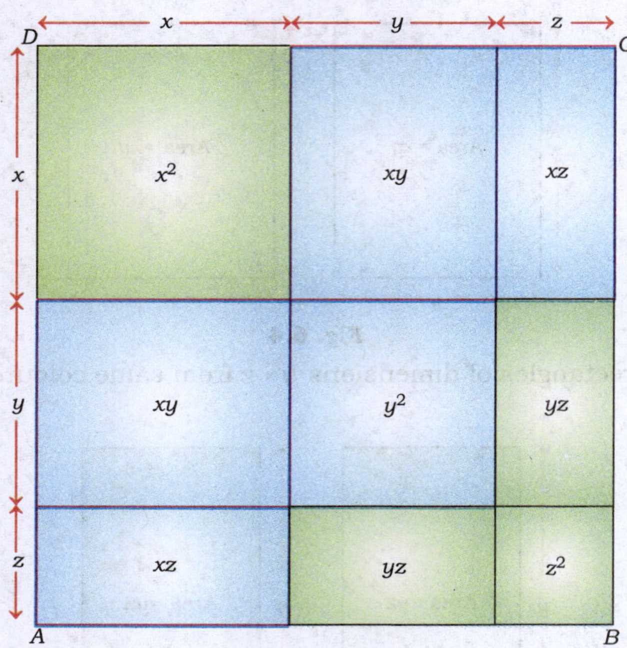

Fig. 6.7

Observation

From Fig. 6.7, it is clear that from the arrangement of squares and rectangles, square *ABCD* of side $(x + y + z)$ units is obtained.

$\therefore$ Area of square $ABCD = (x + y + z)^2$ $\quad$ [$\because$ area of square = (side)^2] ...(i)

Also, area of square $ABCD$ = Sum of the areas of all the squares and rectangles, which are used to make the square *ABCD*

$$= x^2 + y^2 + z^2 + xy + xy + yz + yz + zx + zx \quad \text{...(ii)}$$

$$= x^2 + y^2 + z^2 + 2xy + 2yz + 2zx$$

From Eqs. (i) and (ii), we have

$$(x + y + z)^2 = x^2 + y^2 + z^2 + xy + xy + yz + yz + zx + zx$$

Here, area is in square units.

On actual measurement, we get

$x = ...,$ $\quad$ $y = ...,$ $\quad$ $z = ...,$

So, $\quad$ $x^2 = ...,$ $\quad$ $y^2 = ...,$ $\quad$ $z^2 = ...,$

$2xy = ...,$ $\quad$ $2yz = ...,$ $\quad$ $2zx = ...,$

$x + y + z = ...$

and $\quad$ $(x + y + z)^2 = ...$

Hence, $(x + y + z)^2 = x^2 + y^2 + z^2 + 2xy + 2yz + 2zx$

Result

Identity $(x + y + z)^2 = x^2 + y^2 + z^2 + 2xy + 2yz + 2zx$ has been verified.

Applications

This identity may be used for

1. calculating the square of a number which can be expressed as a sum of three convenient numbers.
2. simplification and factorisation of algebraic expressions.

Viva-Voce

Q.1 What do you mean by a polynomial?

Ans An algebraic expression, in which the variables involved have only non-negative integral power, is called a polynomial.

Q.2 What do you mean by zeroes of a polynomial?

Ans If $p(x)$ is a polynomial, then a real number k is said to be zero of the polynomial $p(x)$, if $p(k) = 0$.

Q.3 What do you mean by a trinomial?

Ans A polynomial with three terms is called a trinomial.

Q.4 Is the expansion of $(x + y + z)^2$, trinomial?

Ans No, because on expanding $(x + y + z)^2$, we get six terms.

Q.5 Is the identity $(a + b + c)^2 = a^2 + b^2 + c^2 + 2ab + 2bc + 2ca$, holds for all real values of a, b, c?

Ans Yes

Q.6 Which identity should be used to expand $(3x - \sqrt{y} + z)^2$?

Ans $(a + b + c)^2 = a^2 + b^2 + c^2 + 2ab + 2bc + 2ca$

Q.7 Write the condition that the three variables in identity $(a + b + c)^2 = a^2 + b^2 + c^2 + 2ab + 2bc + 2ca$ should be written in two variables form $(x + y)^2 = x^2 + y^2 + 2xy$.

Ans $(a + b + c)^2 = a^2 + b^2 + c^2 + 2ab + 2bc + 2ca$ When $a = x$, $b = y$ and $c = 0$, then

$(x + y)^2 = x^2 + y^2 + 2xy$

Q.8 If we take all the variables equal in the identity $(a + b + c)^2 = a^2 + b^2 + c^2 + 2ab + 2bc + 2ca$, then it will give us a cube of one variable. Is it true? Justify your answer.

Ans No, if $a = b = c$ then $(a + b + c)^2 = (a + a + a)^2 = 9a^2$

which is square of one variable.

Activity 7

OBJECTIVE

To verify the algebraic identity $(x+y)^3 = x^3 + y^3 + 3x^2y + 3xy^2$.

Prior Knowledge

1. Concept of cuboid and its volume.
2. Concept of cube and its volume.

Materials Required

1. Acrylic sheets
2. Adhesive/Adhesive tape
3. A pair of scissors
4. Geometry Box
5. Cutter

Theory

1. **Cuboid** A cuboid is a solid bounded by six rectangular plane surfaces. e.g. Match box, brick, box, etc., are cuboid. (see Fig. 7.1)

   Properties of cuboid:

   (i) In a cuboid, there are 6 faces, 12 edges and 8 corners (four at bottom and four at top face) which are called vertices.

   (ii) Opposite faces of a cuboid are equal and parallel.

   $$\text{Volume of cuboid} = lbh$$

   where, l = length, b = breadth and h = height

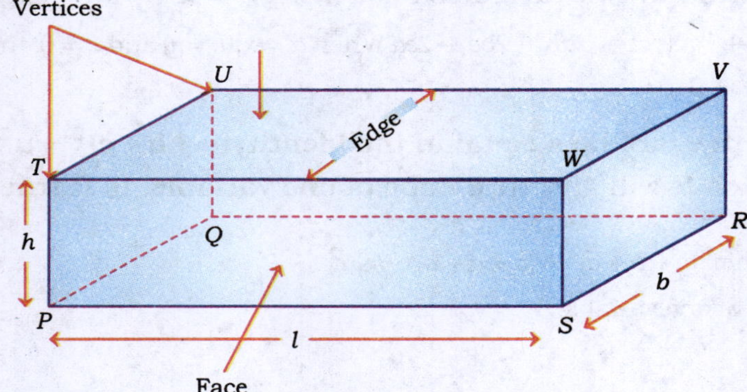

Fig. 7.1

2. **Cube** A cuboid whose length, breadth and height are same, is called a cube. (see Fig. 7.2)

Properties of cube:

(i) In a cube, there are 6 faces, 12 edges and 8 corners (four at bottom and four at top face) which are called vertices.

(ii) All the six faces of a cube are congruent square faces.

(iii) Each edge of a cube have same length.

$$\text{Volume of cube} = a^3$$

where, a is side of cube.

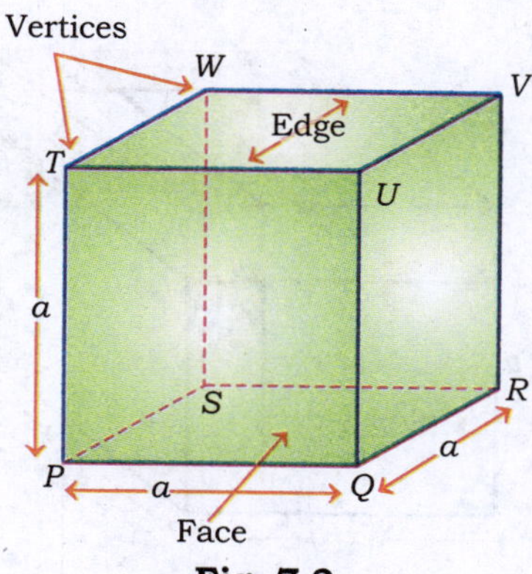

Fig. 7.2

Procedure

1. Cut six squares of equal side x units (say $x = 8$ cm) from acrylic sheet. Paste all of them to form a cube by using adhesive tape/adhesive. (see Fig. 7.3)
2. Cut six squares of equal side y units (say $y = 6$ cm, $y < x$) from acrylic sheet. Paste all of them to form a cube by using adhesive tape/adhesive. (see Fig. 7.4)

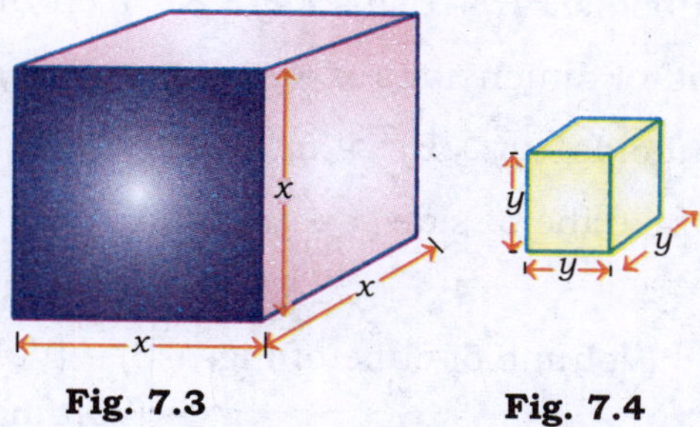

Fig. 7.3 **Fig. 7.4**

3. Also, cut 12 rectangles of length x units and breadth y units and 6 squares of side x units. Paste all of them to form three cuboids. (see Fig. 7.5)

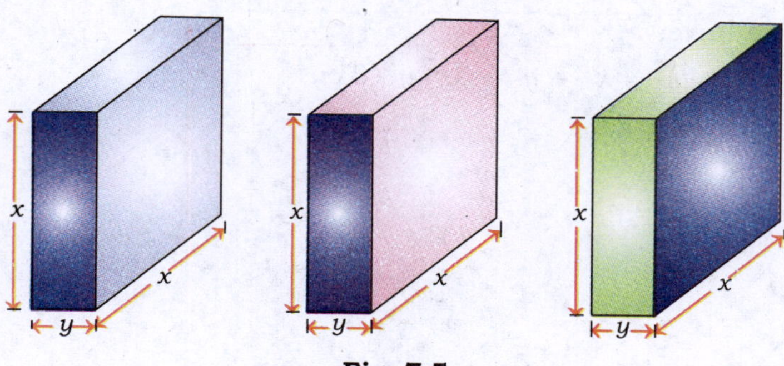

Fig. 7.5

4. Cut 12 rectangles of length x units and breadth y units and 6 squares of side y units. Paste all of them to form another three cuboids. (see Fig. 7.6)

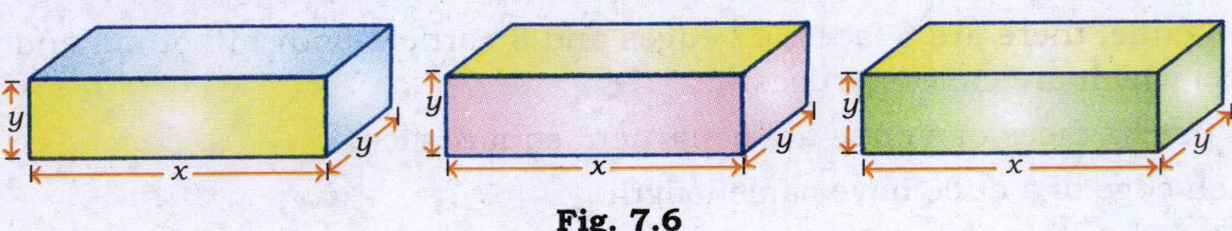

Fig. 7.6

5. Arrange the cubes obtained in Fig. 7.3 and Fig. 7.4 and the cuboids obtained in Fig. 7.5 and Fig. 7.6, as shown in Fig. 7.7.

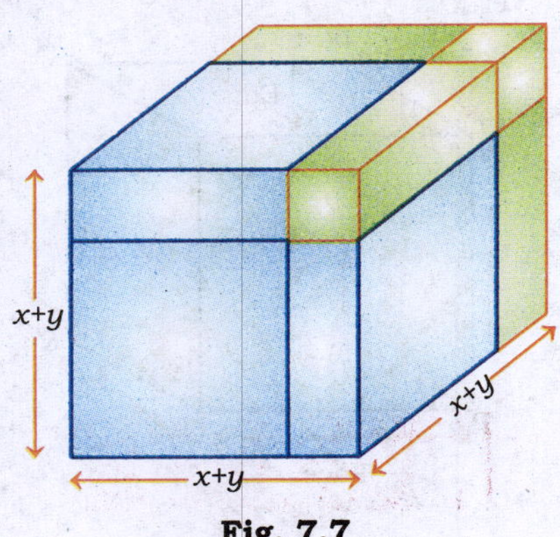

Fig. 7.7

Observation

For Fig. 7.3, volume of cube of side x units = x^3 cu unit

For Fig. 7.4, volume of cube of side y units = y^3 cu unit

For Fig. 7.5, volume of a cuboid of dimensions $x \times x \times y$ units = x^2y cu unit

So, volume of all three such cuboids $x^2y + x^2y + x^2y = 3x^2y$ cu unit

For Fig. 7.6, volume of a cuboid of dimensions $x \times y \times y$ units = xy^2 cu unit

So, volume of all three such cuboids $xy^2 + xy^2 + xy^2 = 3xy^2$ cu unit

In Fig. 7.7, we have obtained the cube of side $(x + y)$ units.

So, volume of cube = $(x + y)^3$ ...(i)

As, volume of cube of Fig. 7.7 = (Volume of cube of Fig. 7.3) + (Volume of cube of Fig. 7.4)
+ (Volume of three cuboids of Fig. 7.5)
+ (Volume of three cuboids of Fig. 7.6)

$\Rightarrow$ $= x^3 + y^3 + 3x^2y + 3xy^2$ ...(ii)

From Eqs. (i) and (ii) we have,

$$(x + y)^3 = x^3 + y^3 + 3x^2y + 3xy^2$$

Here, volume is in cubic units.

On actual measurement, we get

$x = \ldots\ldots\ldots,$ $\quad y = \ldots\ldots\ldots\ldots,$

So, $x^3 = \ldots\ldots\ldots,$ $\quad y^3 = \ldots\ldots\ldots,$

$3x^2y = \ldots\ldots\ldots,$ $\quad 3xy^2 = \ldots\ldots\ldots,$

$(x + y)^3 = \ldots\ldots\ldots$

Hence, $(x + y)^3 = x^3 + y^3 + 3x^2y + 3xy^2$

Result

The algebraic identity $(x + y)^3 = x^3 + y^3 + 3x^2y + 3xy^2$ has been verified.

Applications

The identity is useful for

1. calculating the cube of a number which can be expressed as the sum of two convenient numbers.
2. simplification and factorisation of algebraic expressions.

Viva-Voce

Q.1 Is $(a + b)^3$ a trinomial? Justify.

Ans No, because $(a + b)^3$ has four terms.

Q.2 What is the degree of expansion of polynomial $(x + 2y)^3$?

Ans 3, because the highest power of variable in the expansion of $(x + 2y)^3$ is 3.

Q.3 In the identity $(a + b)^3$, what do you mean by a^3 and $3a^2b$?

Ans a^3 means volume of cube of side a and $3a^2b$ means volume of three cuboids of dimensions a, a and b.

Q.4 What is the maximum number of zeroes that a cubic polynomial can have?

Ans Three

Q.5 What is the expanded form of $(a + b)^3$?

Ans $(a + b)^3 = a^3 + b^3 + 3a^2b + 3ab^2$

Q.6 For evaluating $(101)^3$, which identity would you use?

Ans We should use $(a + b)^3 = a^3 + b^3 + 3a^2b + 3ab^2$ by taking $a = 100$ and $b = 1$.

Q.7 Write the standard form of cubic polynomial in one variable?

Ans $ax^3 + bx^2 + cx + d, a \neq 0$

Activity 8

OBJECTIVE

To verify the algebraic identity $(x - y)^3 = x^3 - y^3 - 3xy(x - y)$.

Prior knowledge

1. Concept of cuboid and its volume.
2. Concept of cube and its volume.

Materials Required

1. Geometry box
2. Acrylic sheet
3. A pair of scissors
4. Adhesive/Adhesive tape
5. Cutter

Theory

1. For concept of cuboid and its volume refer to Activity 7.
2. For concept of cube and its volume refer to Activity 7.

Procedure

1. By using acrylic sheet and adhesive tape/adhesive, make a cube of side $(x - y)$ units, where $x > y$ (say $x = 8$ cm, $y = 2$ cm) (see Fig. 8.1)

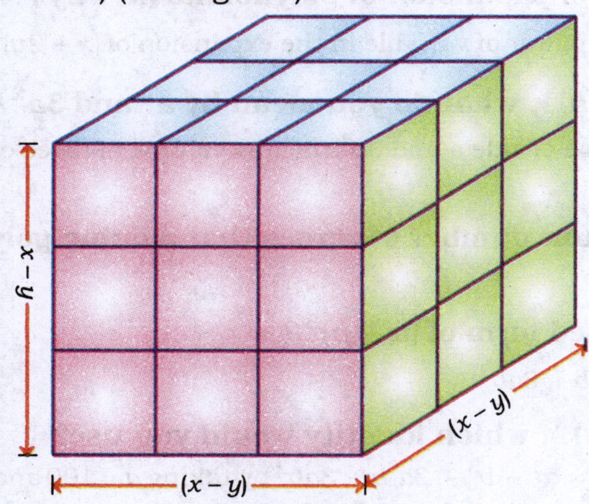

Fig. 8.1

2. By using acrylic sheet and adhesive tape, make three cuboids each of dimensions, $(x - y) \times x \times y$. (see Fig. 8.2)

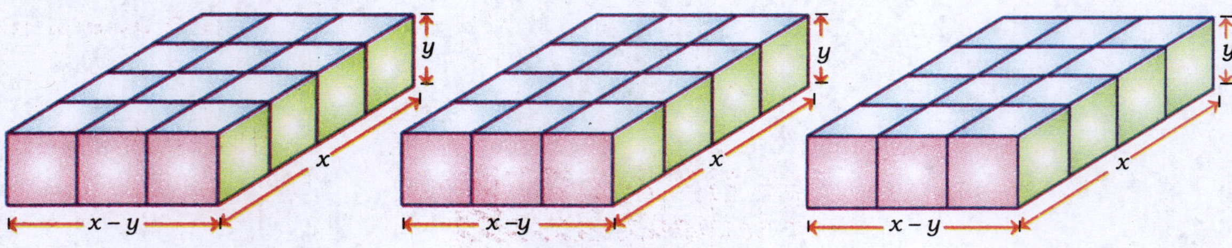

Fig. 8.2

3. By using acrylic sheet and adhesive tape, make a cube of side y units. (see Fig. 8.3)

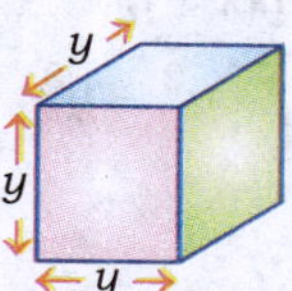

Fig. 8.3

4. Arrange all the cubes and cuboids as shown in Fig 8.4.

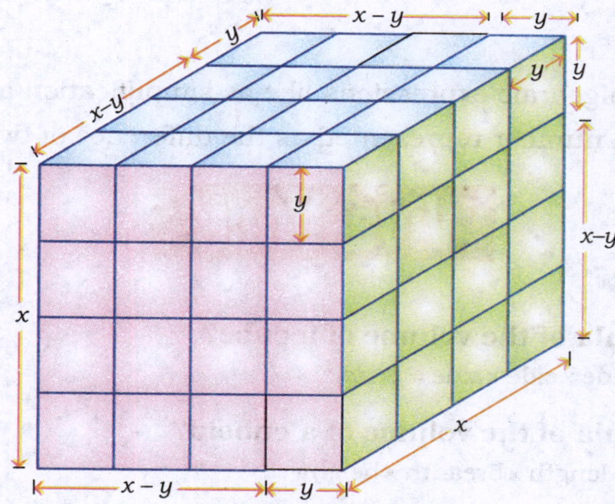

Fig. 8.4

Observation

In Fig. 8.1, volume of the cube of side $(x-y)$ units $=(x-y)^3$

In Fig. 8.2, volume of a cuboid of sides $(x-y)\times x\times y=(x-y)xy$

So, volume of three cuboids $=3\times(x-y)xy$

In Fig. 8.3, volume of the cube of side $y=y^3$

In Fig. 8.4, volume of the solid = Sum of volume of all cubes and cuboids

$$=(x-y)^3+(x-y)\cdot xy+(x-y)\cdot xy+(x-y)\cdot xy+y^3$$

$$=(x-y)^3+3(x-y)\cdot xy+y^3 \qquad \text{...(i)}$$

Also, the obtained solid in Fig. 8.4 is a cube of side x.

Therefore, its volume $=x^3$ ...(ii)

From Eqs. (i) and (ii), we get

$$(x-y)^3+3xy(x-y)+y^3=x^3$$

$$\Rightarrow \quad (x-y)^3=x^3-y^3-3xy(x-y)$$

Here, volume is in cubic units.

By actual measurement,

$x=$ ...... , $y=$ ...... , $x-y=$ ...... ,

So, $x^3=$ ...... , $xy=$ ...... , $y^3=$ ...... ,

$3xy(x-y)=$ ...... , $(x-y)^3=$ ......

Therefore, we observe that

$$(x-y)^3 = x^3 - y^3 - 3xy(x-y)$$

or

$$(x-y)^3 = x^3 - 3x^2y + 3xy^2 - y^3$$

Result

From above observation, the algebraic identity

$(x-y)^3 = x^3 - y^3 - 3xy(x-y)$ or $(x-y)^3 = x^3 - y^3 - 3x^2y + 3xy^2$ has been verified.

Applications

This identity is useful in

1. many operations of algebraic expressions like as simplification and factorisation.
2. calculating cube of a number represented as the difference of two convenient numbers.

Q.1 What is the formula of the volume of a cube?

Ans Volume of a cube = side × side × side = $(side)^3$

Q.2 What is the formula of the volume of a cuboid?

Ans Volume of a cuboid = length × breadth × height

Q.3 How would you expand $a^3 - b^3$ in the terms of $(a-b)^3$?

Ans We know that $(a-b)^3 = a^3 - b^3 - 3ab(a-b)$

$$= a^3 - b^3 - 3a^2b + 3ab^2$$

$$\Rightarrow \quad a^3 - b^3 = (a-b)^3 + 3a^2b - 3ab^2$$

Q.4 Does the resulted value of the product of $(a-b)^2$ and $(a-b)$ is same as $(a-b)^3$? Give reason.

Ans Yes, because $(a-b)^2(a-b) = (a-b)^3 = a^3 - b^3 - 3ab(a-b)$ $[\because A^m \times A^n = (A)^{m+n}]$

Q.5 Which identity would you use to find the cube of 99?

Ans $(a-b)^3 = a^3 - b^3 - 3ab(a-b)$ by putting $a = 100$ and $b = 1$

Q.6 What is the sum of $(a+b)^3$ and $(a-b)^3$?

Ans $(a+b)^3 + (a-b)^3 = a^3 + b^3 + 3a^2b + 3ab^2 + a^3 - b^3 - 3a^2b + 3ab^2 = 2a^3 + 6ab^2$

Activity 9

OBJECTIVE

To verify the algebraic identity $x^3 + y^3 = (x + y)(x^2 - xy + y^2)$.

Prior Knowledge

1. Concept of cuboid and its volume.
2. Concept of cube and its volume.

Materials Required

1. Acrylic sheets
2. Geometry box
3. Adhesive/Cello-tape
4. Cutter
5. A pair scissors

Theory

1. For concept of cuboid and its volume refer to Activity 7.
2. For concept of cube and its volume refer to Activity 7.

Procedure

1. Make a cube of side x units (say $x = 8$ cm) and another cube of side y units (say $y = 5$ cm, $y < x$) by using acrylic sheets and cello-tape/adhesive. (see Fig. 9.1 and 9.2)

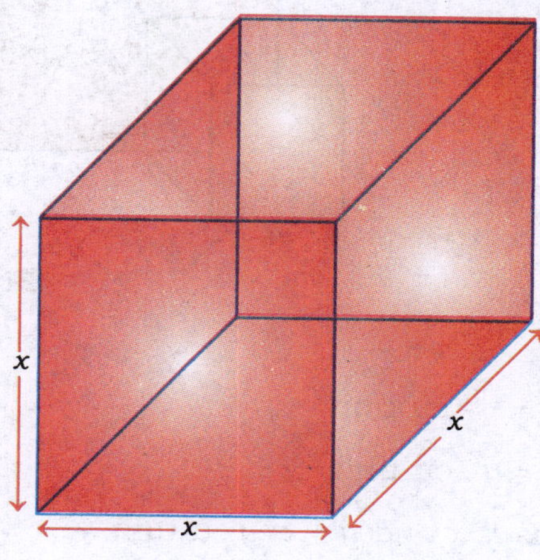

Fig. 9.1

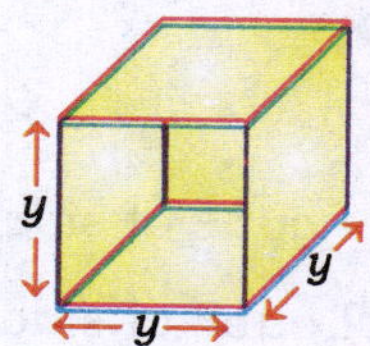

Fig. 9.2

2. Make a cuboid of dimensions $x \times x \times y$ using acrylic sheet and cello-tape/adhesive. (see Fig. 9.3)

3. Make a cuboid of dimensions $x \times y \times y$ using acrylic sheet and cello-tape/adhesive. (see Fig. 9.4)

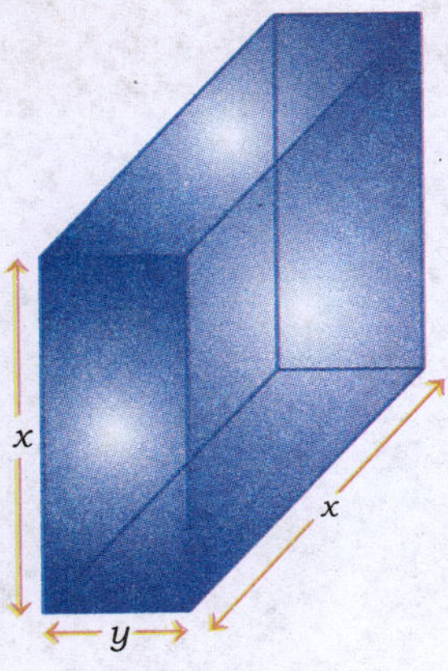

Fig. 9.3

Fig. 9.4

4. Arrange all the cubes and cuboids as shown in Fig. 9.5.
5. Remove cuboids of dimensions $x \times x \times y$ and $x \times y \times y$ from the solid obtained in Fig. 9.5, to get another solid as shown in Fig. 9.6.

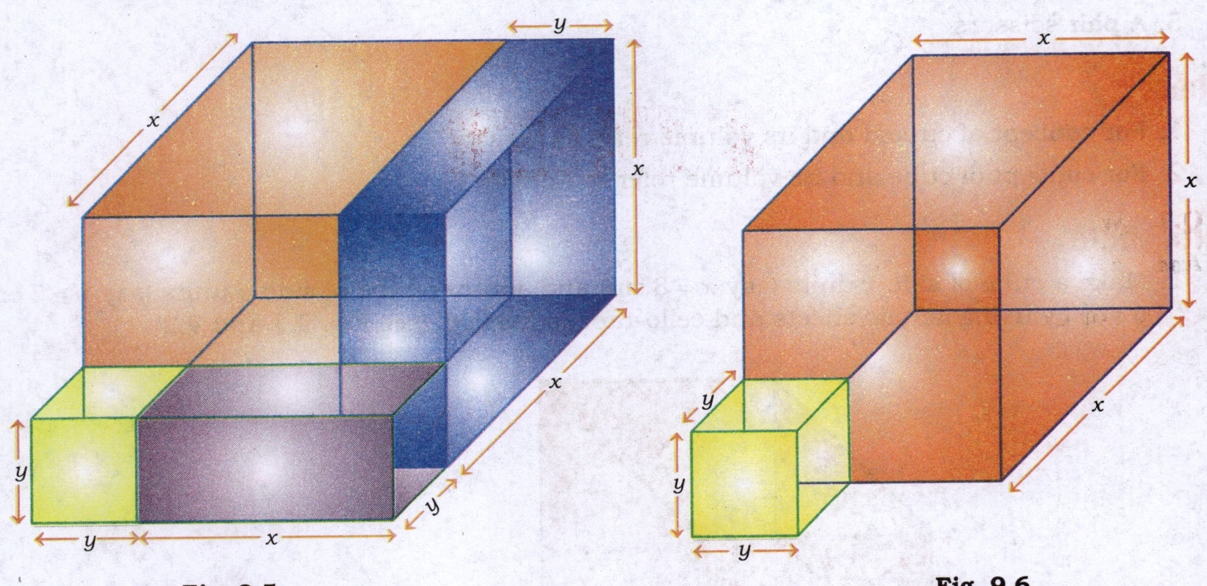

Fig. 9.5

Fig. 9.6

Observation

In Fig. 9.1, volume of cube of side x units $= x^3$ cu unit

In Fig. 9.2, volume of cube of side y units $= y^3$ cu unit

In Fig. 9.3, volume of cuboid of dimensions x, x and $y = x^2y$ cu unit

In Fig. 9.4, volume of cuboid of dimensions x, y and $y = xy^2$ cu unit

Volume of the solid obtained in Fig. 9.5 = Total volume of all cubes and cuboids

$$= x^3 + y^3 + xy^2 + x^2y = x^2(x + y) + y^2(x + y)$$

$$= (x + y)(x^2 + y^2)$$

After removing cuboids of volume x^2y (i.e. $x \times x \times y$) and xy^2 (i.e. $x \times y \times y$) from solid obtained in Fig. 9.5, we get another solid given in fig. 9.6.

So, volume of solid in Fig. 9.6 $= (x+y)(x^2+y^2) - x^2y - xy^2$

$= (x+y)(x^2+y^2) - xy(x+y) = (x+y)(x^2+y^2-xy)$

Also, volume of solid in Fig. 9.6 $= x^3 + y^3$

Hence, $x^3 + y^3 = (x+y)(x^2+y^2-xy)$

Here, volume is in cubic units.

On actual measurement, we get

$x =$ ...... , $y =$ ......,

So, $x^3 =$ ...... , $y^3 =$ ......, $x + y =$ ......,

$x^2 =$ ...... , $y^2 =$ ......, $xy =$ ......,

Hence, $x^3 + y^3 = (x+y)(x^2+y^2-xy)$

Result

The algebraic identity $x^3 + y^3 = (x+y)(x^2+y^2-xy)$ has been verified.

Application

The identity can be used in simplification and factorisation of algebraic expressions.

Viva-Voce

Q.1 What is the condition which satisfy the condition $a^3 + b^3 = 0$?

Ans $a = -b$

Q.2 For evaluating $(90)^3 + (10)^3$, which identity should you follow?

Ans $a^3 + b^3 = (a+b)(a^2 - ab + b^2)$ will be appropriate.

Q.3 How would you express $(a+b)(a^2 - ab + b^2)$ in shortest form?

Ans $a^3 + b^3$

Q.4 What is the degree of an algebraic expression $a^3 + b^3$?

Ans The degree of given algebraic expression is 3.

Q.5 Let *a* and *b* be the edges of two cubes. Is $a^3 + b^3$ equal to the sum of volumes of cubes?

Ans Yes

Q.6 If $(x + y)$ and xy are given, can you find the value of $x^3 + y^3$? Justify your answer.

Ans Yes, we know that $(x+y)^3 = x^3 + y^3 + 3xy(x+y)$

$\Rightarrow \quad x^3 + y^3 = (x+y)^3 - 3xy(x+y)$

By putting $(x + y)$ and xy we can find $(x^3 + y^3)$.

Q.7 Write the expression $8x^3 + 27y^3$ in factor form.

Ans $(2x)^3 + (3y)^3 = (2x+3y)[(2x)^2 + (3y)^2 - 2x \cdot 3y]$ $\quad [\because x^3 + y^3 = (x+y)]$

$= (2x+3y)(4x^2 + 9y^2 - 6xy)$

$= (2x+3y)(4x^2 - 6xy + 9y^2)$

Activity 10

OBJECTIVE

To verify the algebraic identity $x^3 - y^3 = (x - y)(x^2 + xy + y^2)$.

Prior Knowledge

1. Concept cuboid and its volume.
2. Concept of cube and its volume.

Materials Required

1. Acrylic sheets
2. Geometry box
3. A pair of scissors
4. Adhesive/Adhesive tape
5. Cutter

Theory

1. For concept of cuboid and its volume, refer to Activity 7.
2. For concept of cube and its volume, refer to Activity 7.

Procedure

1. Using acrylic sheet, make a cuboid of dimensions $(x - y) \times x \times x$ where $y < x$ (say $x = 8$ cm, $y = 5$ cm). (see Fig. 10.1)
2. Make another cuboid of dimensions $(x - y) \times x \times y$, where $y < x$ using acrylic sheet and adhesive. (see Fig. 10.2).

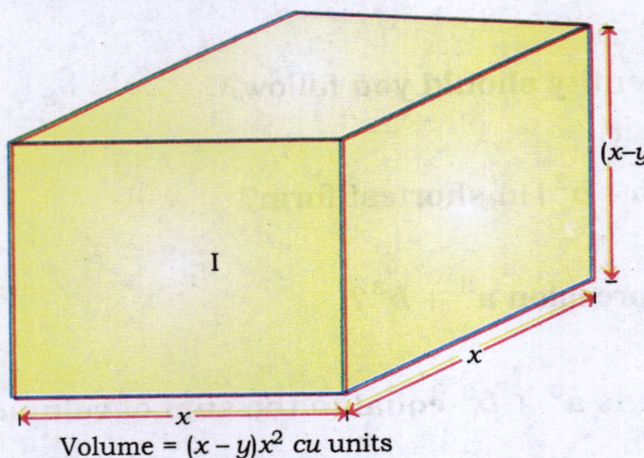

Volume = $(x - y)x^2$ *cu* units

Fig. 10.1

II
y
x
(x − y)

Volume = $(x - y)xy$ *cu* units

Fig. 10.2

3. Now, make one more cuboid of dimensions $(x - y) \times y \times y$ where $y < x$. (see Fig. 10.3)
4. Now, make a cube of dimensions $y \times y \times y$. (see Fig. 10.4)

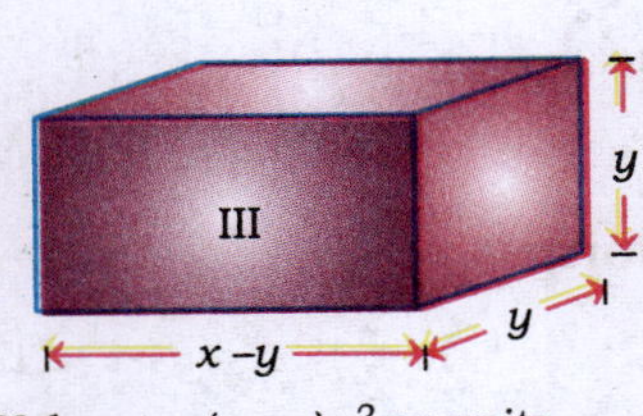

Volume = $(x - y)y^2$ *cu* units

Fig. 10.3

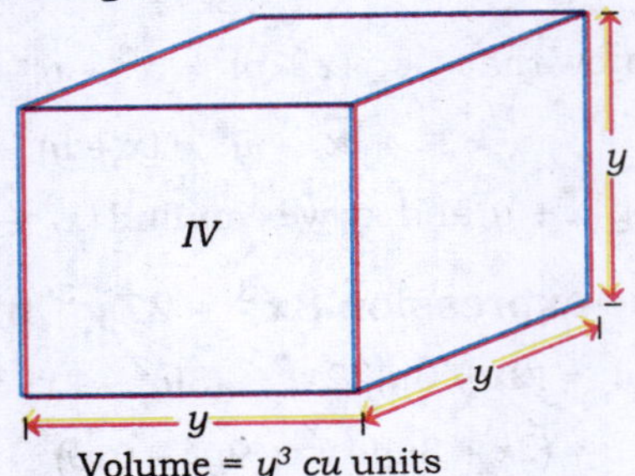

Volume = y^3 *cu* units

Fig. 10.4

5. Arrange the cube and cuboids obtained in Fig. 10.1 to 10.4 to form a solid as shown in Fig. 10.5, which is a cube of side x units.
6. Now, remove a cube of side y units from the solid obtained in Fig. 10.5, thus we obtain a solid as shown in Fig. 10.6.

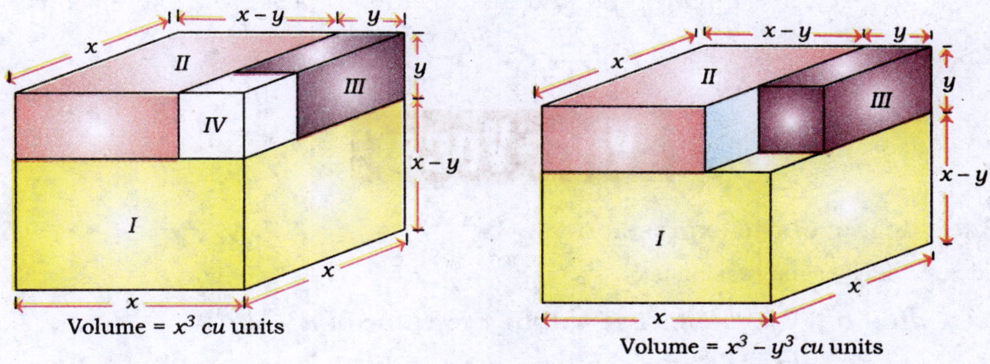

Fig. 10.5 **Fig. 10.6**

Observation

For Fig. 10.1, volume of cuboid $= (x - y) \times x \times x = (x - y)x^2$ cu units.

For Fig. 10.2, volume of cuboid $= (x - y) \times x \times y = (x - y)xy$ cu units.

For Fig. 10.3, volume of cuboid $= (x - y) \times y \times y = (x - y)y^2$ cu units.

For Fig. 10.4, volume of cube $= y^3$ cu units.

For Fig. 10.5, volume of cube = Sum of volume of all cubes and cuboids

$$= [(x - y)x^2 + (x - y)xy + (x - y)y^2 + y^3] \text{ cu units.} \quad ...(i)$$

The cube obtained in Fig. 10.5 has its each side x.

$\therefore$ Its volume = (side)$^3 = x^3$ cu units ...(ii)

From Eqs. (i) and (ii), we get

$$x^3 = (x - y)x^2 + (x - y)xy + (x - y)y^2 + y^3 \quad ...(iii)$$

For Fig. 10.6, volume of solid obtained $= x^3 - y^3$

$$= (x - y)x^2 + (x - y)xy + (x - y)y^2 + y^3 - y^3 \quad \text{[from Eq. (iii)]}$$

$$= (x - y)x^2 + (x - y)xy + (x - y)y^2$$

$$= (x - y)(x^2 + xy + y^2) \text{ cu units}$$

Therefore, $x^3 - y^3 = (x - y)(x^2 + xy + y^2)$

On actual measurement, we get

x = ..., y = ...,

So, x^2 = ..., y^2 = ...,

$(x - y)$ = ..., xy = ...,

x^3 = ..., y^3 = ...

Hence, $x^3 - y^3 = (x - y)(x^2 + xy + y^2)$

Result

The algebraic identity $x^3 - y^3 = (x-y)(x^2 + xy + y^2)$ has been verified.

Application

The identity can be used in simplification and factorisation of algebraic expressions.

Viva-Voce

Q.1 What is degree of the expression $y^3 - x^3$?

Ans The degree of given expression is 3.

Q.2 If $(a^2 + ab + b^2) = 0$, then what will be the value of $a^3 - b^3$?

Ans $\because \quad a^3 - b^3 = (a-b)(a^2 + ab + b^2)$

$\therefore \quad a^3 - b^3 = 0 \qquad [\because a^2 + ab + b^2 = 0]$

Q.3 If $x = y$, then what will be the value of $x^3 - y^3$?

Ans $x^3 - y^3 = x^3 - x^3 = 0 \qquad [\because x = y]$

Q.4 If we replace a by $-a$ and b by $-b$, then what is the expansion of $a^3 - b^3$?

Ans $\therefore$ On replacing a by $-a$ and b by $-b$, we have

$$= (-a)^3 - (-b)^3 = -a^3 + b^3$$

$$\Rightarrow \quad b^3 - a^3 = (b-a)(b^2 + a^2 + ab)$$

Q.5 Write the expression $x^3 - y^3$ in terms of $(x-y)$ and xy.

Ans Since, $(x-y)^3 = x^3 - y^3 - 3xy(x-y)$

$\therefore \quad x^3 - y^3 = (x-y)^3 + 3xy(x-y)$

Q.6 If $x^2 + \dfrac{1}{x^2} = 27$, then what is value of $x^3 - \dfrac{1}{x^3}$?

Ans $\left(x - \dfrac{1}{x}\right)^2 = x^2 + \dfrac{1}{x^2} - 2 = 27 - 2 = 25$

$\therefore \quad x - \dfrac{1}{x} = \sqrt{25} = 5 \qquad$ [taking positive square root]

Now, $x^3 - \dfrac{1}{x^3} = \left(x - \dfrac{1}{x}\right)\left(x^2 + \dfrac{1}{x^2} + 1\right) = 5 \times (27 + 1) = 140$

Activity 11

OBJECTIVE

To find the values of abscissae and ordinates of various points given in a cartesian plane.

Prior Knowledge

1. Knowledge of cartesian coordinate system.
2. To locate/plot a point in cartesian plane.

Materials Required

1. Cardboard
2. White paper
3. Graph paper with various given points
4. Geometry box
5. A pair of scissors
6. Glue

Theory

1. **Cartesian Coordinate System**

   The system used to describe the position of a point in a plane, is called **cartesian system.**

   In cartesian system, there are two perpendicular directed straight lines XX' and YY' which intersect at point O, such that line XX' is the **horizontal line** and YY' is the **vertical line**, as shown in figure 11.1 (a).

   The point of intersection of these lines is called **origin** and it is denoted by O. The horizontal line XOX' is called **X-axis** and the vertical line YOY' is called **Y-axis**. Directions OX and OY are called the **positive directions** of X-axis and Y-axis, respectively and directions OX' and OY' are called the **negative directions** of X-axis and Y-axis, respectively.

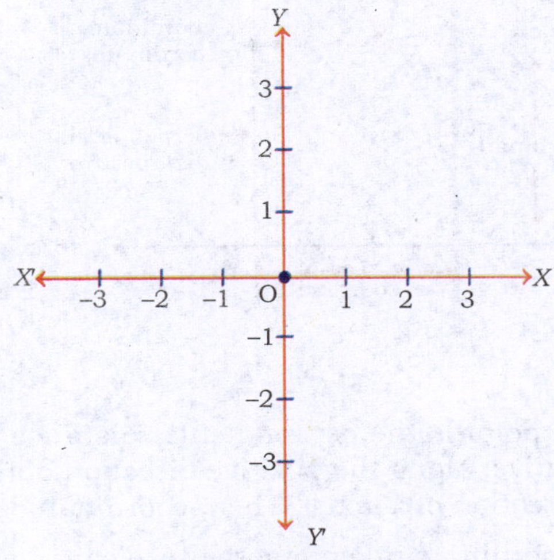

Fig. 11.1 (a)

2. **Quadrants**

The axes divide the plane into four parts called quadrants. The quadrants are numbered I, II, III and IV anti-clockwise from *OX*. Thus,

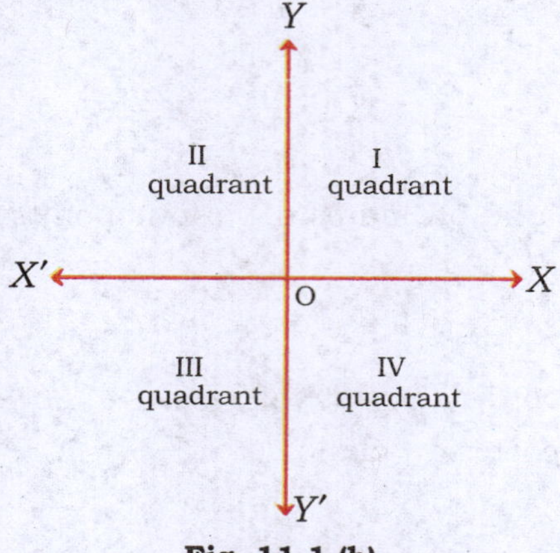

Fig. 11.1 (b)

(i) *XOY* is called I quadrant

(ii) *X′OY* is called II quadrant

(iii) *X′OY′* is called III quadrant

(iv) *XOY′* is called IV quadrant

3. **Coordinates of a Point in Cartesian Plane**

To locate a point in the cartesian plane, its perpendicular distances from *X*-axis and *Y*-axis are required, these distances are called **coordinates** of the point. Each point in cartesian plane has two coordinates; *x*-coordinate and *y*-coordinate.

(i) The *x*-coordinate of a point is the perpendicular distance from the *Y*-axis measured along the *X*-axis (positive, along the positive direction of the *X*-axis and negative, along the negative direction of *X*-axis). The *x*-coordinate is also called the **abscissa**.

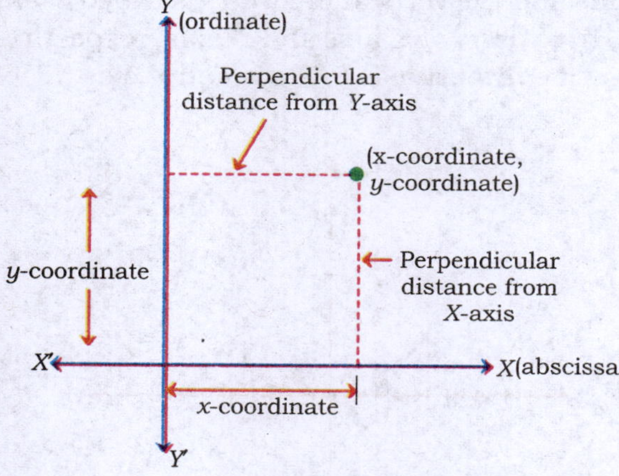

Fig. 11.2

(ii) The *y*-coordinate of a point is the perpendicular distance from the *X*-axis measured along the *Y*-axis (positive, along the positive direction of the *Y*-axis and negative, along the negative direction of *Y*-axis). The *y*-coordinate is also called the **ordinate**.

x-coordinate and *y*-coordinate taken together are called **cartesian coordinates** or **coordinates of a point** and are denoted by (x, y). Here, the *x*-coordinate comes first and after this *y*-coordinate comes. (x, y) is also called an **order pair**.

The order of x and y is important in (x, y). Position of (y, x) will be different from (x, y).

Sign Conventions

The sign of coordinates of a point in a quadrant are given in following table.

Quadrant	Nature of *X*-axis and *Y*-axis	Sign of *x*-abscissa	Sign of *y*-ordinate	Coordinates of a point
I	$x > 0,\ y > 0$	+	+	(+, +)
II	$x < 0,\ y > 0$	–	+	(–, +)
III	$x < 0,\ y < 0$	–	–	(–, –)
IV	$x > 0,\ y < 0$	+	–	(+, –)

Procedure

1. Take a cardboard of suitable size and paste a white paper on it.
2. Now, paste the graph paper with various points drawn on it in the middle of white paper.
3. Now, look at the graph paper and the points whose abscissae and ordinates are to be found.

Observation

If L is a point plotted on graph paper and we have to find the abscissa and ordinate of point L.

Draw perpendiculars LE and LD from L to X-axis and Y-axis, respectively.

$LD = 1$ units (distance from Y-axis, i.e. x-coordinate or abscissa)

$LE = 9/2$ units (distance from X-axis, i.e. y-coordinate or ordinate)

As, point L lies in second quadrant.

So, the coordinates of L are $\left(-1, \dfrac{9}{2}\right)$. or $(-1, 4 \cdot 5)$.

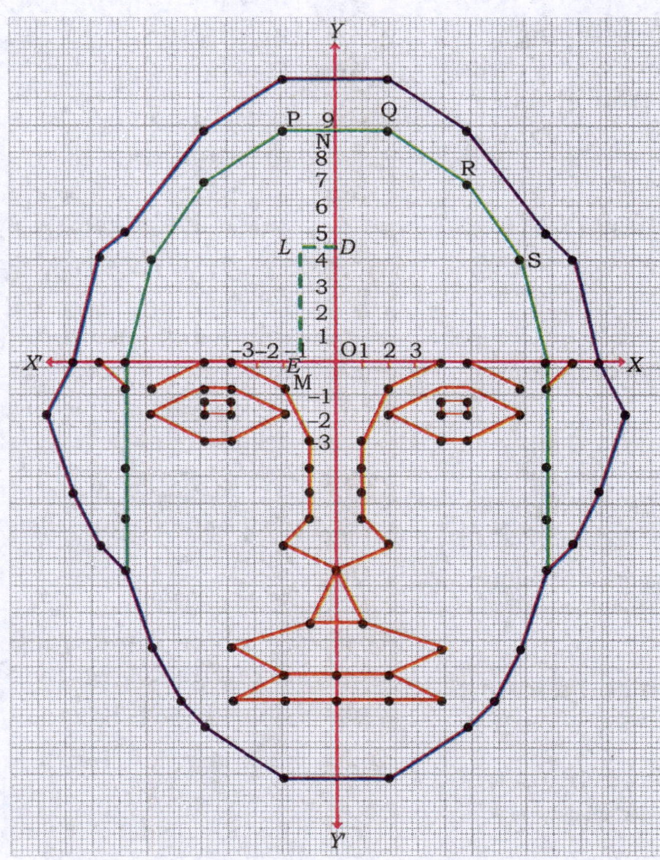

Note *Care should be taken while reading the coordinates, otherwise the location of the object will differ.*

Fill the given table for different points on the given graph.

Points	Abscissa	Ordinate	Quadrant	Coordinates
M				
N				
P				
⋮				

Result

The coordinates of the points plotted on the graph paper have been found.

Application

This activity is very useful in locating the position of a particular country/city or a place on map.

Viva-Voce

Q.1 What do you understand by a cartesian system?

Ans The system used to describe the position of a point in a plane, is called cartesian system.

Q.2 What is the ordinate of point lying in third quadrant at a distance of 2 units from X-axis and 5 units from Y-axis?

Ans – 2, because in third quadrant y-coordinate is negative.

Q.3 What type of graph do you get for $y = -2$?

Ans A straight line parallel to X-axis at a distance of 2 units from origin below the X-axis.

Q.4 What is the image of (– 3, – 1) in 2nd quadrant?

Ans (– 3, 1)

Q.5 What type of graph do you get for $x = -2$?

Ans A straight line parallel to Y-axis at a distance of 2 units from origin lying in the left side of Y-axis.

Q.6 A point (–2, –6) lies in which quadrant?

Ans Third quadrant

Q.7 Abscissa and ordinate of a point can never be equal. Is it true or false.

Ans False, as a point can be equidistant from X-axis and Y-axis.

Q.8 In cartesian system, X-axis and Y-axis divide the graph paper in how many quadrants?

Ans Four quadrants

Q.9 Is the point (–7, 2), same as point (2, – 7)? Justify.

Ans No, in coordinates of a point, their order matters, so (–7, 2) is not same as (2, – 7).

Q.10 Find the new coordinates of a point (2, 3), when we rotate the axes at 180° in anti-clockwise direction.

Ans When we rotate the axes, the positive X and Y-axes will become negative. So, the new coordinates will be (–2, –3).

Q.11 In cartesian plane, the angle between two axes is not always 90°. Is it true or false.

Ans False, the angle between two axes is always 90°.

Q.12 In which quadrant a point lies whose ordinate is negative?

Ans Either III or IV quadrant.

Q.13 Is it correct that if any point lies on the X-axis, then the y-coordinate will be zero?

Ans Yes, because the distance from X-axis is zero.

Activity 12

OBJECTIVE

To verify experimentally that if two lines intersect each other, then

(i) the vertically opposite angles are equal.

(ii) the sum of two adjacent angles is 180°.

(iii) the sum of all the four angles is 360°.

Prior Knowledge

1. Basic knowledge of lines and angles.
2. Pair of angles, adjacent angles, linear pair of angles and vertically opposite angles.

Materials Required

1. Cardboard
2. White sheet of paper
3. A full protractor
4. A nail
5. Two transparent strips marked as PQ and RS
6. Adhesive

Theory

1. **Lines and Angles**

(i) **Line Segment** A part of a line with two end points, is called a line segment. Line segment PQ is denoted by $\overline{PQ}$.

P ——————— Q

Line segment PQ

Fig. 12.1

A line segment has a definite length, which can be measured. The line segment PQ is the same thing as the line segment QP.

(ii) **Angle** The figure formed by two rays with the same initial point, is called an angle. In Fig. 12.2, the common initial point Q is known as the **vertex** of the angle and the rays ($\overrightarrow{QP}$ and $\overrightarrow{QR}$) forming the angle are called its **arms** or **sides**.

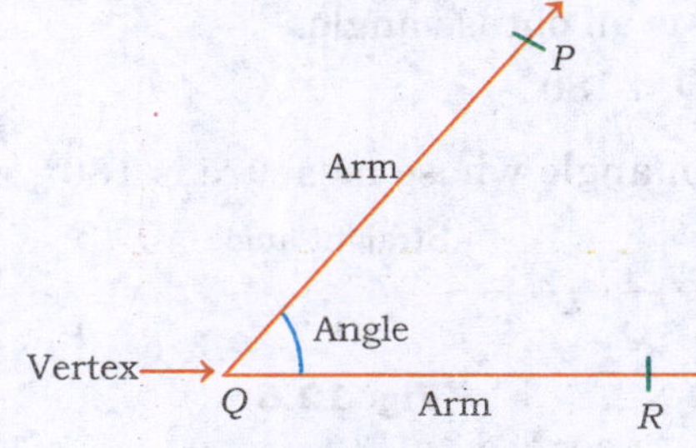

Fig. 12.2

There are different types of angles such as acute angle, right angle, obtuse angle, straight angle, reflex angle and complete angle, which are discussed below :

(a) **Acute Angle** An angle whose measure is more than 0° but less than 90°, is called an acute angle.

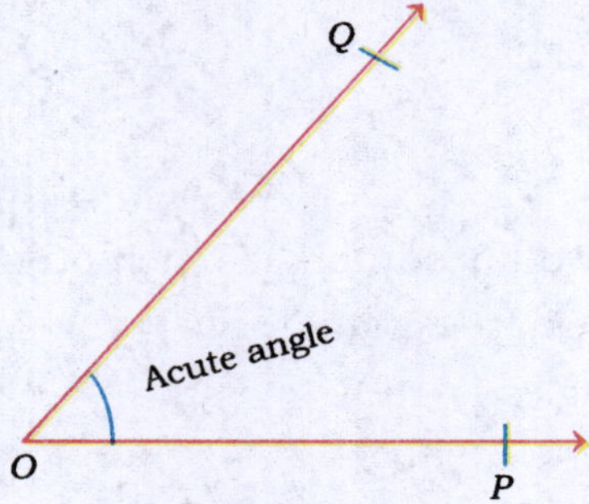

Fig. 12.3

In Fig. 12.3, $\angle POQ$ is an acute angle.

Since, $0° < \angle POQ < 90°$

(b) **Right Angle** An angle whose measure is 90°, is called a right angle.

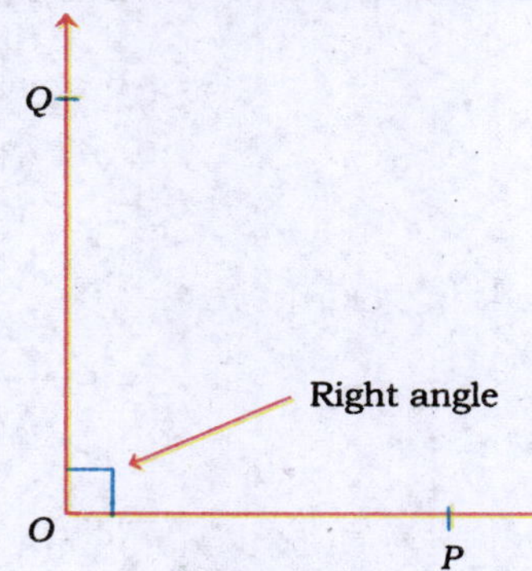

Fig. 12.4

In Fig. 12.4, $\angle POQ$ is a right angle and $OQ \perp OP$.

(c) **Obtuse Angle** An angle whose measure is more than 90° but less than 180°, is called an obtuse angle.

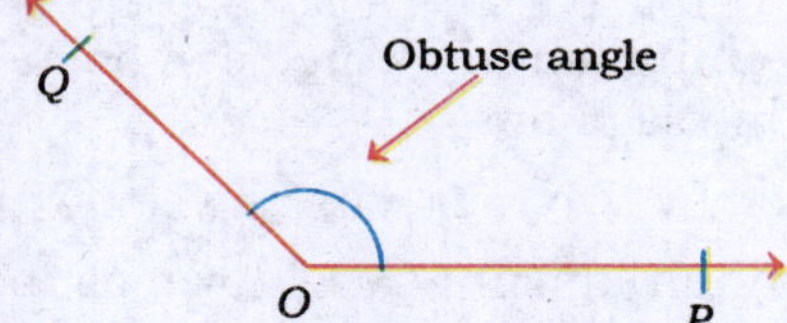

Fig. 12.5

In Fig. 12.5, $\angle POQ$ is an obtuse angle.

Since, $90° < \angle POQ < 180°$

(d) **Straight Angle** An angle whose measure is 180°, is called a straight angle.

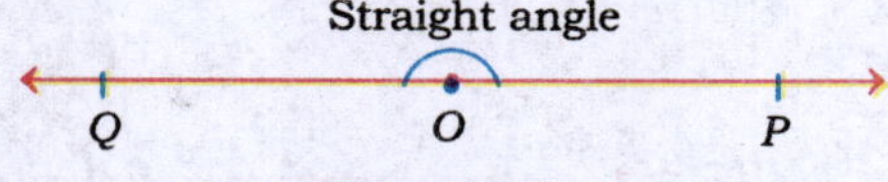

Fig. 12.6

In Fig. 12.6, $\angle POQ = 180°$ is a straight angle.

A straight angle has two right angles.

(e) **Reflex Angle** An angle whose measure is more than 180° but less than 360°, is called a reflex angle.

In Fig. 12.7 and Fig. 12.8, $\angle POQ$ and $\angle DEF$ are reflex angles.

- $180° < \text{reflex } \angle POQ < 360°$

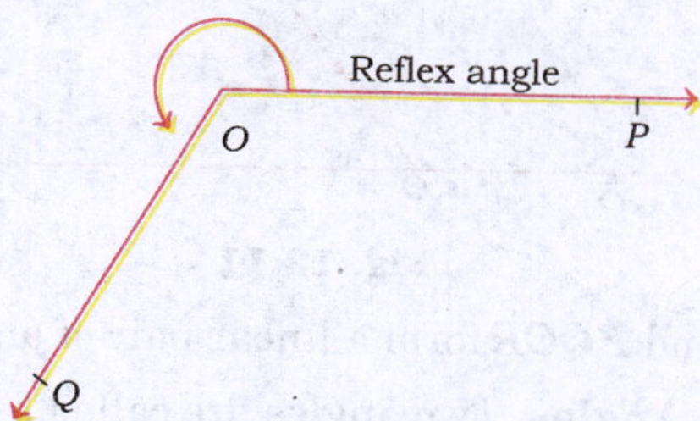

Fig. 12.7

- $180° < \text{reflex } \angle DEF < 360°$

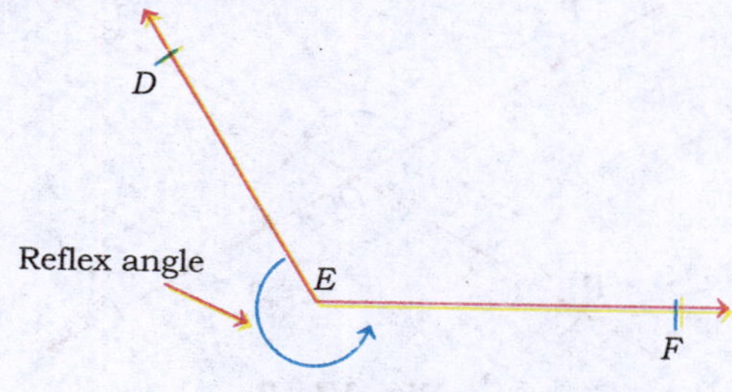

Fig. 12.8

(f) **Complete Angle** An angle whose measure is 360°, is called a complete angle.

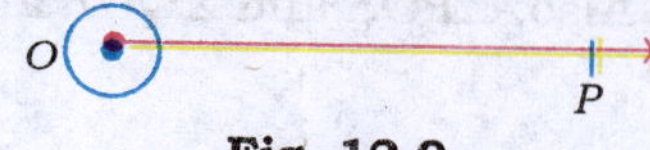

Fig. 12.9

In Fig. 12.9, $\angle POP = 360°$ is a complete angle.

2. **Pair of Angles**

There are some relations between the angles which are described below:

(i) **Adjacent Angles** Two angles are called adjacent angles, if

(a) they have a common vertex,

(b) they have a common arm and

(c) their non-common arms are on different sides of the common arm.

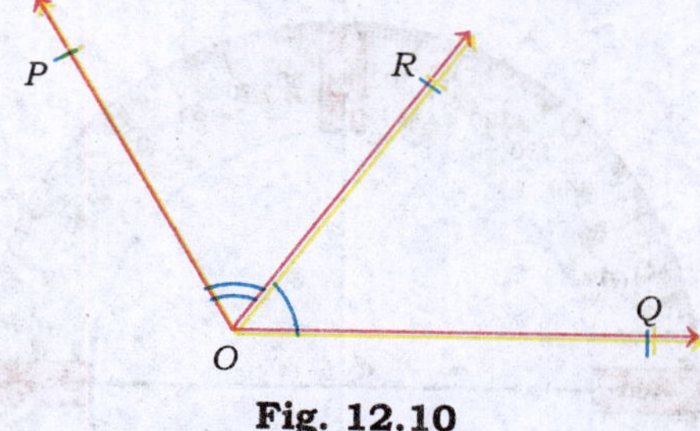

Fig. 12.10

In Fig. 12.10, $\angle POR$ and $\angle ROQ$ are adjacent angles because these angles have a common vertex O, a common arm OR and non-common arms OP and OQ.

When two angles are adjacent, then their sum is always equal to the angle formed by the two non-common arms. So, here $\angle POQ = \angle POR + \angle ROQ$.

Note *Here, $\angle POQ$ and $\angle POR$ are not adjacent angles because their non-common arms OR and OQ lie on the same side of the common arm OP.*

(ii) **Linear Pair of Angles** If the non-common arms of two adjacent angles form a line, then adjacent angles are called linear pair of angles.

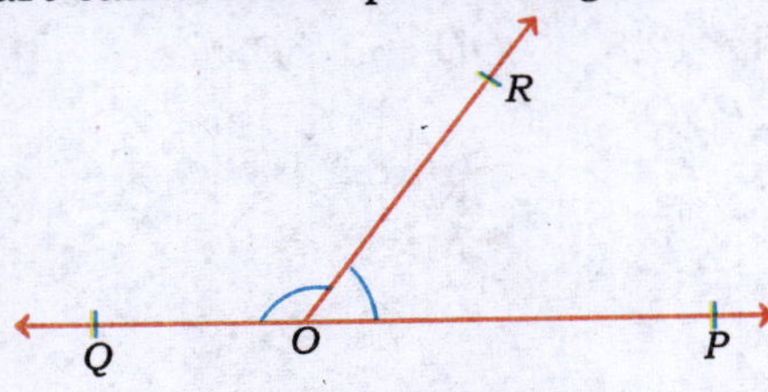

Fig. 12.11

In Fig. 12.11, $\angle POR$ and $\angle QOR$ form a linear pair of angles.

(iii) **Vertically Opposite Angles** Two angles are called a pair of vertically opposite angles, if their arms form two pairs of opposite rays. In other words, when two lines intersect each other at a point, then there are two pairs of vertically opposite angles.

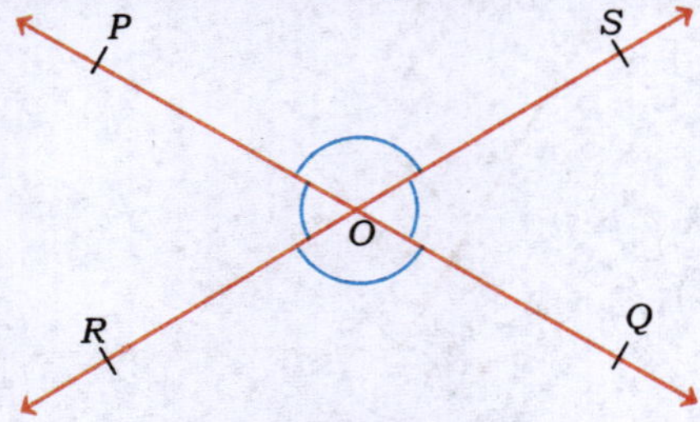

Fig. 12.12

In Fig. 12.12, lines PQ and RS intersect each other at O. So, $\angle POR$ and $\angle QOS$ are vertically opposite angles. Also, $\angle POS$ and $\angle QOR$ are vertically opposite angles.

Procedure

1. Take a cardboard of suitable size and by using adhesive, paste a white sheet of paper on it.
2. Also, paste a full protractor (0° to 360°) with the help of adhesive on the cardboard. (see Fig. 12.13)
3. Mark the centre of protractor as O.
4. Now, make a hole in the middle of both transparent strips which contain two intersecting lines.
5. Fix both strips at O by putting a nail. (see Fig. 12.13)
6. Set the different positions of the strips PQ and RS, and measure the angles $\angle POS$, $\angle POR$ $\angle ROQ$ and $\angle SOQ$.

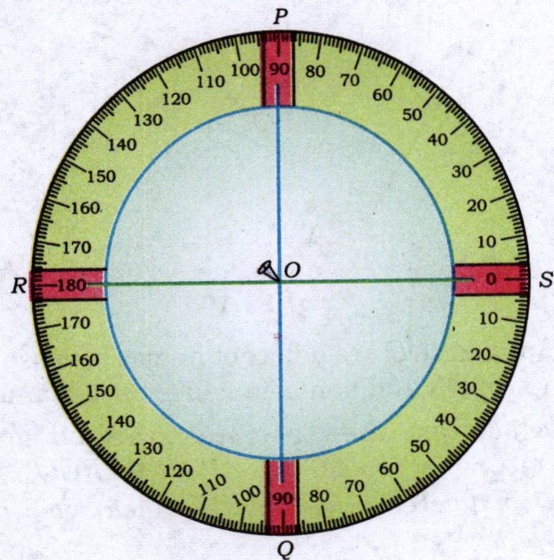

Fig. 12.13

Observations

1. Observe the adjacent and the vertically opposite angles formed in different positions of the strips.
2. Compare vertically opposite angles formed by the two lines in the strips in different positions.
3. Cheek the relationship between the vertically opposite angles.
4. Check that the vertically opposite angles $\angle POS$, $\angle ROQ$ and $\angle ROP$, $\angle QOS$ are equal.
5. Compare the pairs of adjacent angles and check that $\angle ROP + \angle SOP = 180°$.
6. Find the sum of all the four angles formed at the point O and see that the sum is equal to 360°.

In one position of the strips, by actual measurement of angles

1. $\angle POS =$ ......, $\angle POR =$ ......
   $\angle ROQ =$ ......, $\angle QOS =$ ......
   Hence, $\angle POS = \angle ROQ$ and $\angle POR = \angle QOS$ (vertically opposite angles)
2. $\angle POR + \angle POS =$ ...... , $\angle POR + \angle QOR =$ ...... ,
   $\angle ROQ + \angle QOS =$ ......, $\angle POS + \angle QOS =$ ...... (linear pairs)
3. $\angle POS + \angle POR + \angle ROQ + \angle QOS =$ ...... (angles formed at a point)

Results

We have verified experimentally that if two lines intersect each other, then

1. the vertically opposite angles are equal.
2. the sum of two adjacent angles is 180°.
3. the sum of all the four angles is 360°.

Application

These properties are very useful in proving some theorems and properties of geometrical figures.

Viva-Voce

Q.1 What is the measure of a straight angle?
Ans 180°

Q.2 If the two adjacent angles are supplementary, then what does that mean?
Ans It means that they form a linear pair. or sum of two angles is 180°.

Q.3 Define reflex angle?
Ans An angle which is greater than 180° but less than 360° is called a reflex angle.

Q.4 If the angles are complementary, then what does that mean?
Ans Sum of the two angles is 90°.

Q.5 What is the measure of the angle made at the centre of the circle?
Ans 360°

Q.6 If two angles are vertically opposite angles, where the measure of one of the angles is 30°, then what is the measure of other angle?
Ans 30° because vertically opposite angles are equal.

Q.7 If out of two angles of linear pair, one is 60°, then what is the measure of other angle?
Ans In a linear pair, sum of both angles is 180°, so if one angle is 60°, then other angle is $180° - 60° = 120°$.

Q.8 What is the angle between two parallel lines?
Ans 0°

Q.9 What is the supplement of an obtuse angle?
Ans Acute angle

Activity 13

OBJECTIVE

To verify experimentally the different criteria for congruency of triangles using triangle cut outs.

Prior Knowledge

1. Concept of congruency of figures.
2. Different criteria for congruency of two triangles.

Materials Required

1. Cardboard
2. A pair of scissors/cutter
3. White paper
4. Geometry box
5. Coloured glazed papers
6. Adhesive

Theory

1. **Congruent Figures** Two figures are said to be congruent, if they are of same shape and of same size ('congruent' means equal in all respects).

   e.g. Two circles of the same radii and two squares of the same sides are congruent.

   Congruency of Triangles Two triangles are congruent, if all the sides and angles of a triangle are equal to the corresponding sides and angles of the other triangle.

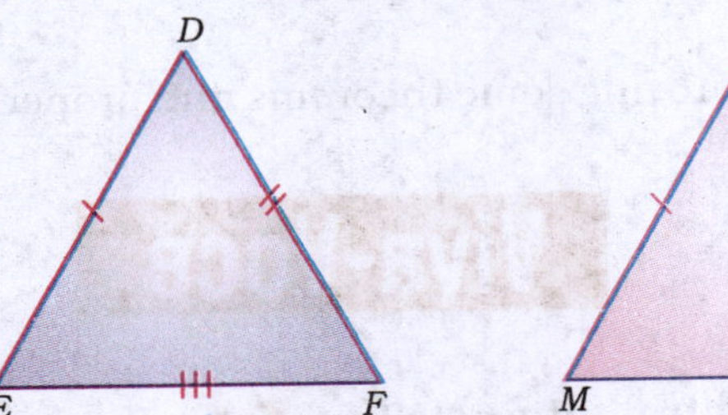

Fig. 13.1

   If ΔDEF is congruent to ΔLMN, then we write $\Delta DEF \cong \Delta LMN$. Here, '$\cong$' is the sign of congruency.

   In congruent triangles, corresponding parts are equal and we write it in short **'CPCT'**, i.e. corresponding parts of congruent triangles.

2. **Criterion for Congruency of Two Triangles**

   There are five different criteria for the two triangles to be congruent.

   (i) SSS (Side-Side-Side) **criterion** If three sides of a triangle are equal to the corresponding three sides of an another triangle, then the two triangles are congruent.

   (ii) SAS (Side-Angle-Side) **criterion** Two triangles are congruent, if two sides and the included angle of a triangle are equal to the corresponding two sides and the included angle of the other triangle.

   (iii) ASA (Angle-Side-Angle) **criterion** Two triangles are congruent, if two angles and the included side of one triangle are equal to the corresponding two angles and the included side of the other triangle.

(iv) **AAS** (Angle-Angle-Side) **criterion** Two triangles are congruent, if two angles and a non-included side of a triangle are equal to the corresponding angles and the side of another triangle.

(v) **RHS** (Right angle-Hypontenuse-Side) **criterion** In two right angled triangles, the hypotenuse and one side of one right angled triangle are equal to the hypotenuse and corresponding side of the other right angled triangle, then the two right angled triangles are congruent.

Procedure

1. Take a cardboard of suitable size and by using adhesive, paste a white paper on it.
2. Cut out a pair of ΔBCD and ΔEFG from glazed paper such that $BC = FE$, $CD = FG$ and $BD = EG$. (see Fig. 13.2)

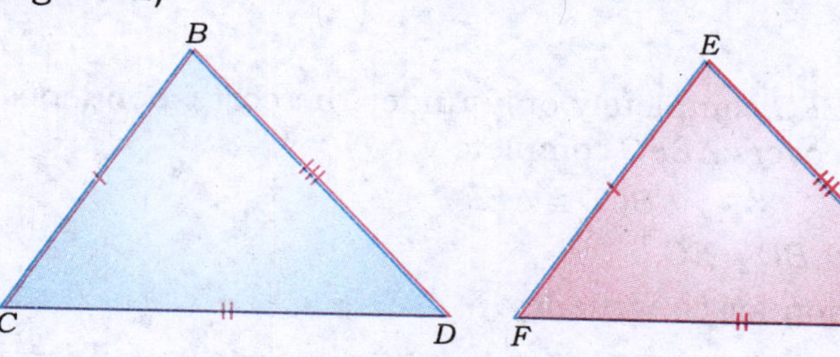

Fig. 13.2

3. Make a pair of ΔHIJ and ΔKLM on glazed paper such that $HI = KL$, $HJ = KM$ and $\angle H = \angle K$ and cut them out. (see Fig. 13.3)

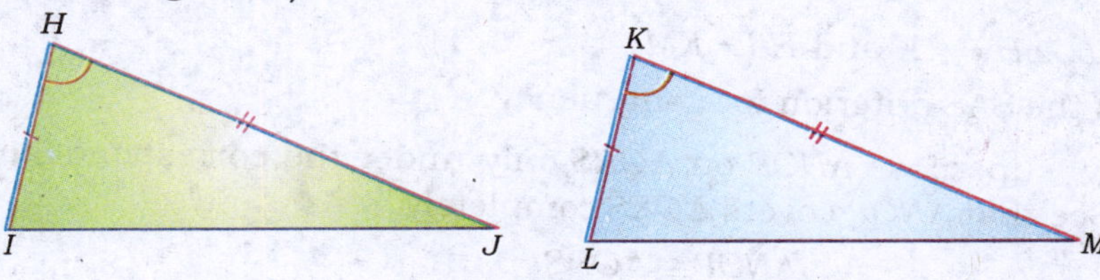

Fig. 13.3

4. Make a pair of ΔNOP and ΔQRS on glazed paper such that $OP = RS$, $\angle O = \angle R$ and $\angle P = \angle S$ and cut them out. (see Fig. 13.4)

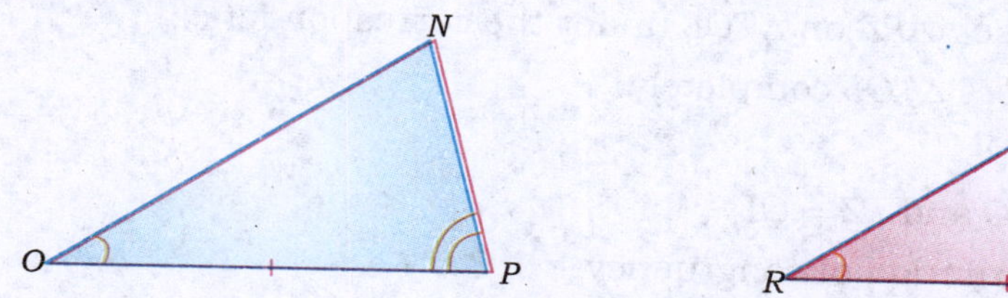

Fig. 13.4

5. Make a pair of ΔAPZ and ΔTQL on glazed paper such that $\angle A = \angle T$, $\angle P = \angle Q$ and $PZ = QL$

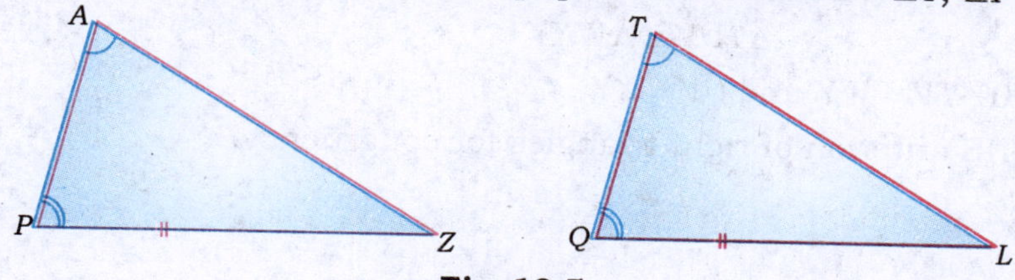

Fig. 13.5

and let them out. (see Fig. 13.5)

6. Make two right angle ΔTUV and ΔWXY from glazed paper such that $TV = WY$, $UV = XY$ and $\angle U = \angle X = 90°$. (see Fig. 13.6)

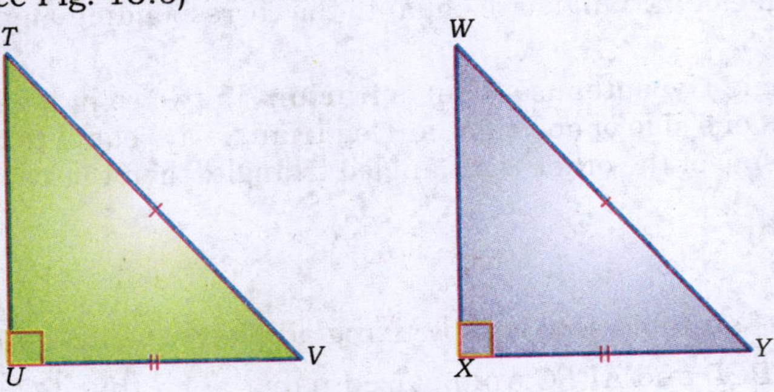

Fig. 13.6

Observation

1. Superpose ΔBCD on ΔEFG completely only under the correspondence $B \leftrightarrow E$, $C \leftrightarrow F$ and $D \leftrightarrow G$. See that ΔBCD covers ΔEFG completely.

   Hence, $\Delta BCD \cong \Delta EFG$

   if $BC = EF$, $CD = FG$ and $BD = EG$

   which is the SSS criterion for congruency.

2. Similarly, superpose ΔHIJ on ΔKLM completely only under the correspondence $H \leftrightarrow K$, $I \leftrightarrow L$ and $J \leftrightarrow M$. See that ΔHIJ covers ΔKLM completely.

   Hence, $\Delta HIJ \cong \Delta KLM$

   if $HI = KL$, $\angle H = \angle K$ and $HJ = KM$

   which is the SAS criterion for congruency.

3. Similarly, superpose ΔNOP on ΔQRS only under the correspondence $N \leftrightarrow Q$, $O \leftrightarrow R$ and $P \leftrightarrow S$. See that ΔNOP covers ΔQRS completely.

   Hence, $\Delta NOP \cong \Delta QRS$

   if $\angle O = \angle R$, $OP = RS$ and $\angle P = \angle S$

   which is the ASA criterion for congruency.

4. Similarly, superpose ΔAPZ on ΔTQL under the correspondence $A \leftrightarrow T$, $P \leftrightarrow Q$ and $Z \leftrightarrow L$. See that ΔAPZ covers ΔTQL completely.

   Hence, $\Delta APZ \cong \Delta TQL$

   if $\angle A = \angle T$, $\angle P = \angle Q$ and $PZ = QL$

   which is the AAS criterion of congruency.

5. Similarly, superpose ΔTUV on ΔWXY only under the correspondence $T \leftrightarrow W$, $U \leftrightarrow X$ and $V \leftrightarrow Y$. See that ΔTUV covers ΔWXY completely.

   Hence, $\Delta TUV \cong \Delta WXY$

   if $\angle U = \angle X = 90°$, $TV = WY$ and $UV = XY$

   which is the RHS criterion of right triangles for congruency.

By actual measurement,

1. In the pair of ΔBCD and ΔEFG,

$BC = EF =$ .... , $CD = FG =$ .... , $BD = EG =$ .... ,

$\angle B =$ .... , $\angle C =$ .... , $\angle D =$ .... ,

$\angle E =$ .... , $\angle F =$ .... , $\angle G =$ .... ,

Hence, $\Delta BCD \cong \Delta EFG$

2. In the pair of ΔHIJ and ΔKLM,

$HI = KL =$ .... , $HJ = KM =$ .... , $\angle H = \angle K$

$IJ =$ .... , $LM =$ .... , $\angle I =$ .... ,

$\angle L =$ .... , $\angle J =$ .... , $\angle M =$ .... ,

Hence, $\Delta HIJ \cong \Delta KLM$

3. In the pair of ΔNOP and ΔQRS,

$OP = RS =$ .... , $\angle O = \angle R =$ .... , $\angle P = \angle S =$ .... ,

$NO =$ .... , $QR =$ .... , $NP =$ .... ,

$QS =$......... , $\angle Q =$ .... , $\angle M =$ ....

Hence, $\Delta NOP \cong \Delta QRS$

4. In the pair of ΔAPZ and ΔTQL

$\angle A = \angle T =$ ...., $\angle P = \angle Q =$ ...., $PZ = QL =$ ....,

$AP =$ ...., $TQ =$ ...., $AZ =$ ....,

Hence, $\Delta APZ \cong \Delta TQL$

5. In the pair of ΔTUV and ΔWXY,

hypotenuse TV = hypotenuse WY = ...

$\angle X = \angle U = 90°$ .... , $TU =$ .... ,

$WX =$ .... ,

$\angle T =$ .... , $\angle W =$ .... ,

$\angle V =$ .... , $\angle Y =$ .... ,

Hence, $\Delta TUV \cong \Delta WXY$

Result

Using triangle cut outs, we have verified experimentally the different criteria for congruence of triangles.

Applications

These criteria are useful in

1. solving many problems in geometry.
2. practical problems such as finding width of a river without crossing it.

Viva-Voce

Q.1 What do you mean by congruent figures?

Ans Two figures are congruent, if they are of the same shape and same size.

Q.2 In a triangle, the smallest side is always opposite to the smallest angle. Is it true or false?

Ans True

Q.3 Is there any AAA congruency criterion for triangles?

Ans No

Q.4 Are the sides opposite to equal angles of a triangle unequal?

Ans No, side opposite to equal angles in a triangle are always equal.

Q.5 Are congruent triangles similar?

Ans Yes

Q.6 What is CPCT?

Ans CPCT stands for Corresponding Parts of Congruent Triangles.

Q.7 What do you mean by the RHS congruence rule for triangles?

Ans According to the RHS congruence rule, in two right angled triangles, if the hypotenuse and one side of one right angled triangle are equal to the hypotenuse and corresponding side of the other right angled triangle, then the two right angled triangles are congruent.

Q.8 If two triangles are congruent. Does they have different perimeters?

Ans No, both have equal perimeters.

Q.9 In two triangles ABC and DEF, if $AB = DE$ and $BC = EF$, then what is the third necessary condition to prove them congruent?

Ans Either $AC = DF$ or $\angle B = \angle E$

Q.10 In ΔABC and ΔDEF, if $\angle A = \angle D$ and $\angle C = \angle F$, then what is the third necessary condition to prove them congruent?

Ans $AC = DF$

Activity 14

OBJECTIVE

To verify that the angle subtended by an arc of a circle at the centre is double the angle subtended by it at any point on the remaining part of the circle.

Prior Knowledge

1. Concept of circle and terms related to it.
2. Angle subtended by an arc.

Materials Required

1. Coloured drawing sheets
2. Cardboard
3. Geometry box
4. White paper
5. Adhesive
6. Transparent sheet
7. Cutter/A pair of scissors

Theory

1. The collection of all the points in a plane, which are at a fixed distance from a fixed point in the plane, is called a **circle**. The fixed point is called the **centre** of the circle, the line segment joining the centre and any point on the circle is called **radius of circle**.
2. The length of the complete circle is called its **circumference**.
3. A line segment joining any two points on the circumference of circle is called a **chord** of the circle.
4. A chord which passes through the centre of the circle is called a **diameter** of the circle.

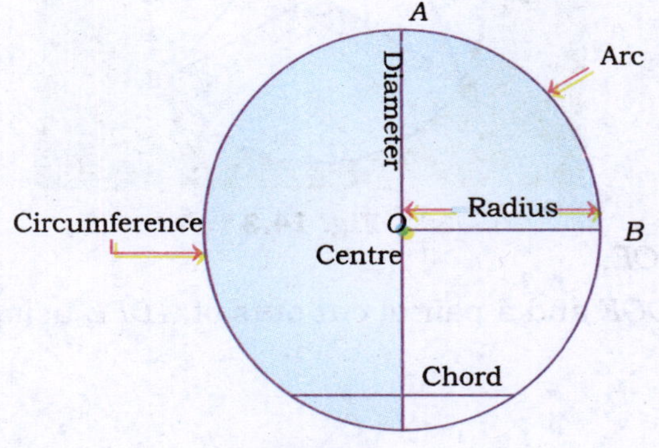

Fig. 14.1

5. A piece of a circumference of circle between any two points is called an **arc**.

6. **Angle Subtended by an Arc of a Circle**

Consider a circle with centre at O and $\overset{\frown}{DE}$ be its arc. Here, $\angle DOE$ is the angle subtended by arc DE ($\overset{\frown}{DE}$) at the centre of the circle.

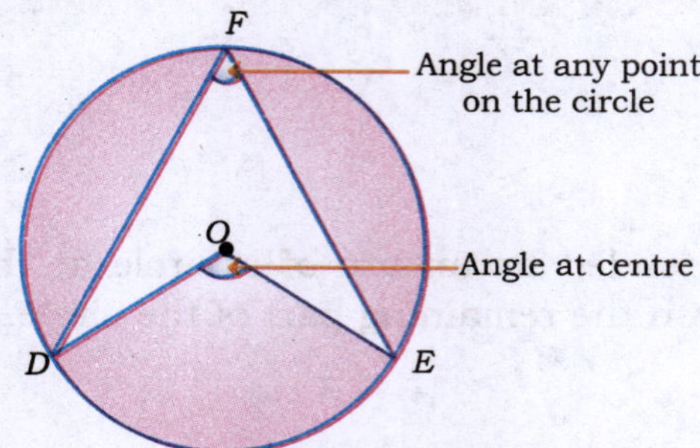

Fig. 14.2

Also, $\angle DFE$ is the angle subtended by arc DE ($\overset{\frown}{DE}$) at a point F on the remaining part of the circle.

Procedure

1. Take a rectangular piece of cardboard of suitable size and by using adhesive, paste a white paper on it.
2. Cut out a circle of any radius with centre O from drawing sheet and paste it on white paper on the cardboard.
3. Take a pair of points D and E on the circle to obtain the arc DE. (see Fig. 14.3)
4. To obtain the angle subtended by arc DE at centre O, join the points D and E to the centre O. (see Fig. 14.3)
5. Take a point F on the remaining part of circle, join it to points D and E to get $\angle DFE$ subtended by arc DE at point F on the remaining part of circle. (see Fig. 14.3)

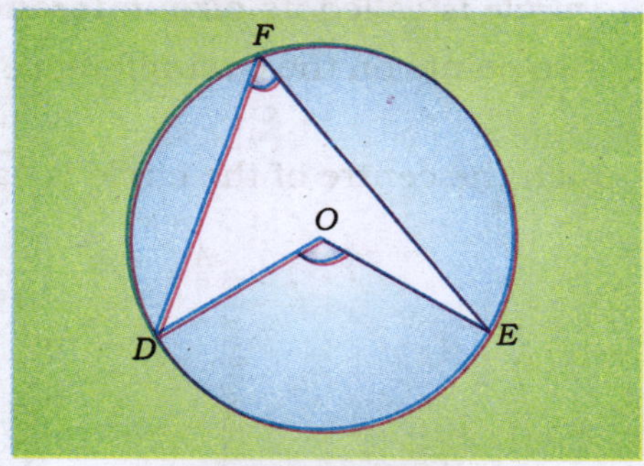

Fig. 14.3

6. Mark $\angle DFE$ and $\angle DOE$.
7. Make a cut out of $\angle DOE$ and a pair of cut outs of $\angle DFE$ using transparent sheet. (see Fig. 14.4)

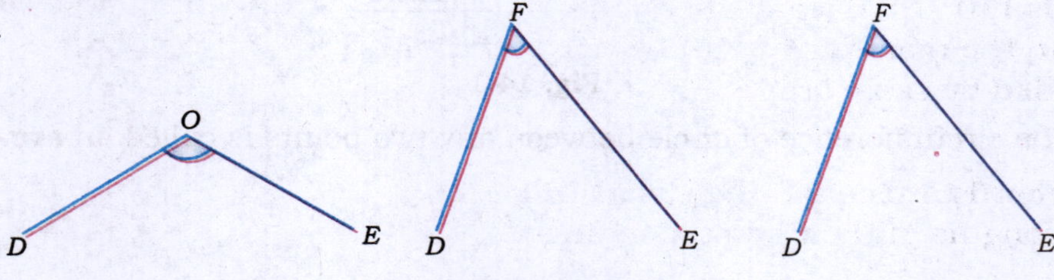

Fig. 14.4

8. Now, place the pair of cut outs of $\angle DFE$ on the cut out of $\angle DOE$, adjacent to each other. (see Fig. 14.5)

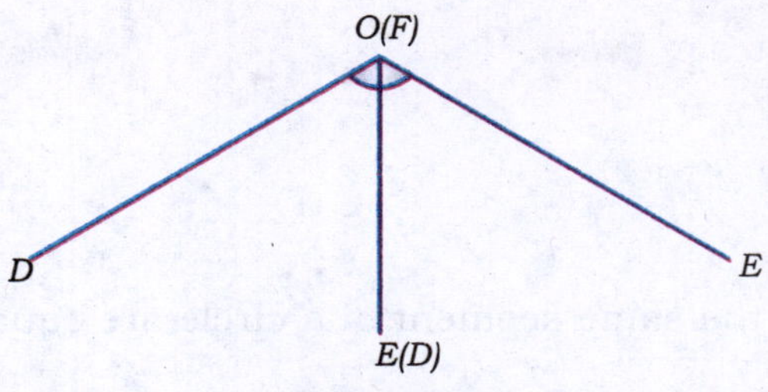

Fig. 14.5

Observation

In the fig 14.5, we see that pair of cut outs of $\angle DFE$ completely overlap the cut out of $\angle DOE$.

Hence, $\angle DOE = 2\angle DFE$

By actual measurement, $\angle DOE =$ …… ., $\angle DFE =$ …… .

Hence, $\angle DOE = 2(\angle DFE)$

Result

We find that the angle subtended by an arc at the centre is double the angle subtended by it at any point on the remaining part of the circle.

Application

The property is used in proving many other important results such as opposite angles of a cyclic quadrilateral are always supplementary angles and angles in the same segment of a circle are always equal.

Viva-Voce

Q.1 How many circles can pass through three non-collinear points?

Ans There is only one such circle.

Q.2 What is the diameter?

Ans The chord which passes through the centre of circle is known as the diameter of circle.

Q.3 Of the two chords of a circle, the one which is nearer to centre is longer. Is it true or false?

Ans True

Q.4 If the angle subtended by an arc at centre is 110°, then what will be the angle on the remaining part of circle subtended by same arc?

Ans 55°

Q.5 If two chords are equal, then what will be the lengths of their corresponding arcs?

Ans For equal chords, the lengths of their corresponding arcs are always equal.

Q.6 If the angles subtended by the chords of a circle at centre are equal, then what is the relation between two chords?

Ans Both chords will be of equal length.

Q.7 What is the name of arc of a circle which substends a right angle at any point of the circle?

Ans Semi-circle.

Q.8 What is the measurement of the angle made in semi-circle?

Ans 90°

Q.9 What is the longest chord of circle?

Ans Diameter

Q.10 What will be the distance of two equal chords from the centre?

Ans Both chords are at equal distance from the centre.

Activity 15

OBJECTIVE

To verify that the angles in the same segment of a circle are equal.

Prior Knowledge

1. Concept of circle and terms related to it.
2. Segment of a circle and angles subtended on it.

Materials Required

1. Coloured glazed papers
2. A pair of scissors
3. Drawing sheet
4. Geometry box
5. Sketch pens
6. Adhesive
7. Transparent sheet

Theory

1. For concept of circle and terms related to it, refer to Activity 14.
2. The region between a chord and either of its arcs is called a **segment** of the circular region or simply a segment of the circle. This chord is called the base of the segment.

   The segment formed by minor arc along with chord, is called **minor segment** and the segment formed by major arc is called the **major segment**. (see. Fig 15.1)

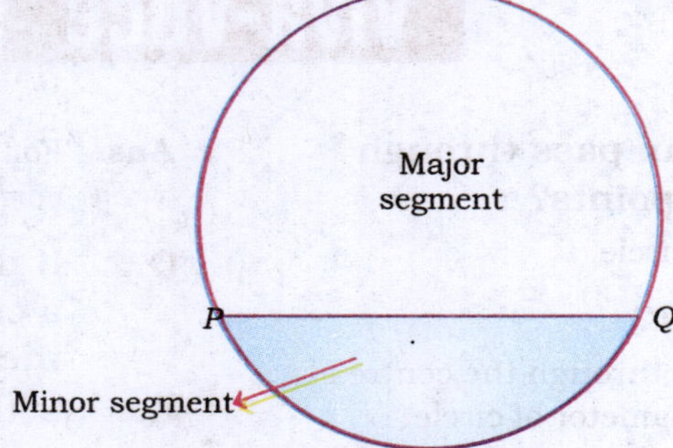

Fig. 15.1

If O is the centre of the circle, PQ is an arc and S and R are two points on the remaining part of circle. Arc PQ subtends two equal angles, $\angle PSQ$ and $\angle PRQ$ in the same segment of the circle. (see Fig. 15.2)

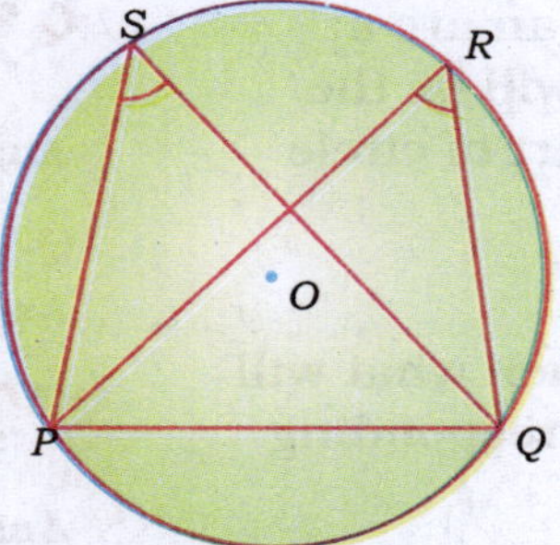

Fig. 15.2

Procedure

1. Take a piece of cardboard of suitable size and paste a drawing sheet on it.
2. From the sheet of glazed paper, cut out a circle of any radius with centre *O*. (see Fig. 15.3)
3. Paste the cut out of a circle on white sheet on the cardboard.
4. To form chord *DE*, take two points *D* and *E* on the circle and join them. (see Fig. 15.4)

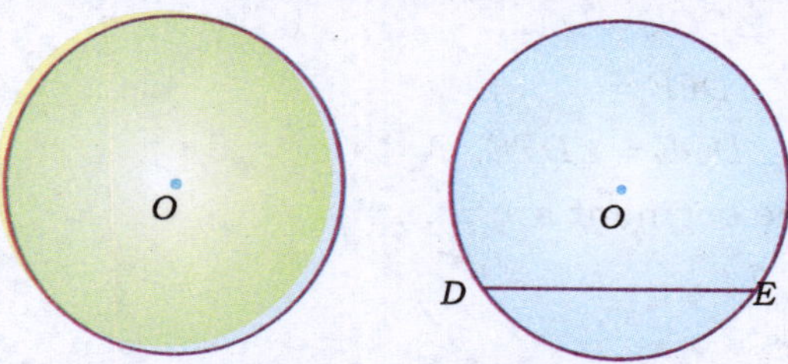

Fig. 15.3 **Fig. 15.4**

5. Take a pair of points *G* and *F* on the circle in the same segment and join *DG*, *GE*, *FE* and *FD*. (see Fig. 15.5)

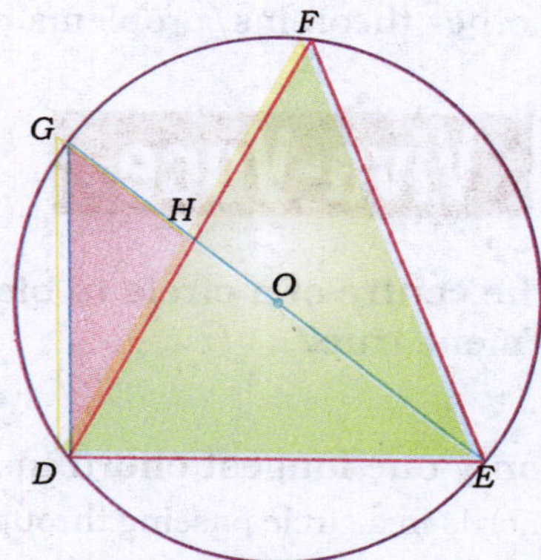

Fig. 15.5

6. Now, take replicas of the $\angle DGE$ and $\angle DFE$ using transparent sheet. (see Fig. 15.6)

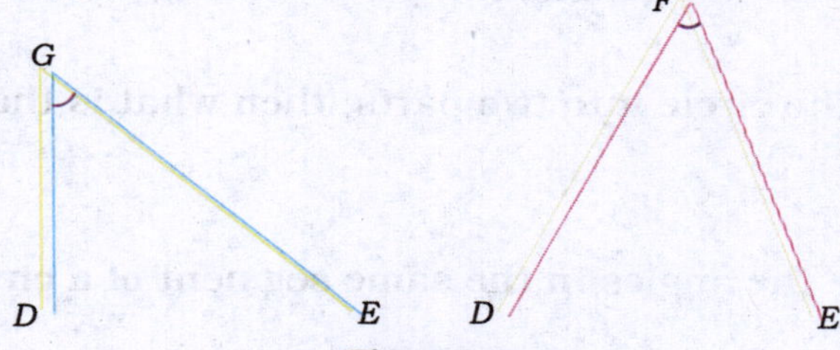

Fig. 15.6

7. Put the cut outs of $\angle DGE$ and $\angle DFE$ on each other such that vertex *G* falls on vertex *F* (see Fig. 15.7).

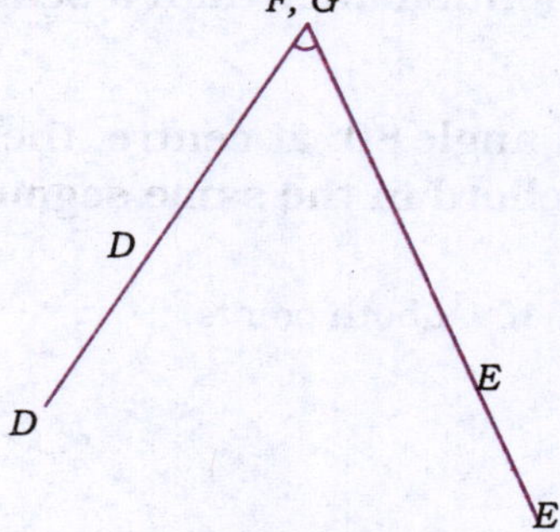

Fig. 15.7

Observation

In the Fig. 15.7, we see that $\angle DGE$ completely covers $\angle DFE$.

Hence, $\angle DGE = \angle DFE$

On actual measurement, we get

$\angle DGE = ...,$

$\angle DFE = ...,$

So, $\angle DGE = \angle DFE.$

Hence, the angles in the same segment are ....

Result

We have verified that the angles are equal in the same segment of a circle.

Application

This result can be used in proving other theorems/problems of geometry related to circles.

Viva-Voce

Q.1 'The line drawn through the centre of a circle to bisect a chord is perpendicular to the chord'. Is this statement true?

Ans Yes

Q.2 Is it correct that there is only one longest chord in a circle? Justify your answer.

Ans No, there are infinite longest chords in a circle passing through the centre and each of them is equal to the diameter of the circle.

Q.3 What do you mean by the minor segment of a circle?

Ans A chord divides a circle into two parts and the part containing the minor arc is called the minor segment.

Q.4 If a chord divides the circle into two parts, then what is that part called which contains major arc?

Ans Major segment

Q.5 How will you relate the angles in the same segment of a circle?

Ans Angles will be equal.

Q.6 Does equal chords of a circle subtend different angles at the centre?

Ans No, because equal chords subtended equal angles at the centre.

Q.7 What is the angle in a segment smaller than a semi-circle.

Ans Obtuse angle

Q.8 If a chord AB subtended an angle 80° at centre, then what will be the measure of angles subtended by same chord in the same segment of the circle at point P and Q?

Ans Chord AB subtended an angle of 40° at both points.

Activity 16

OBJECTIVE

To verify that the opposite angles of a cyclic quadrilateral are supplementary.

Prior Knowledge

1. Knowledge about the supplementary angles, linear pair axiom and interior opposite angles.
2. Concept of cyclic quadrilateral.

Materials Required

1. Cardboard
2. White paper
3. Drawing sheet
4. Geometry box
5. A pair of scissors
6. Sketch pens
7. Adhesive
8. Transparent sheet

Theory

1. Two angles are said to be supplementary, if the sum of their measures is 180°.

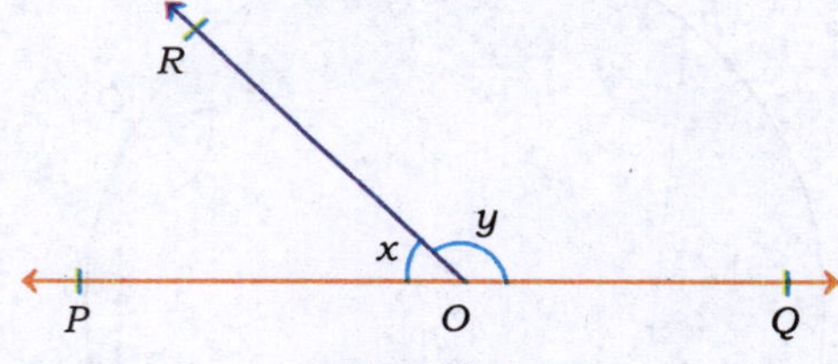

Fig. 16.1

In Fig 16.1, $\angle POR$ and $\angle QOR$ are **supplementary angles** if and only if $\angle POR + \angle QOR = 180°$ i.e. $x + y = 180°$

2. If a ray stands on a line, then the sum of two adjacent angles so formed is 180°, i.e. the sum of the linear pair is 180°.

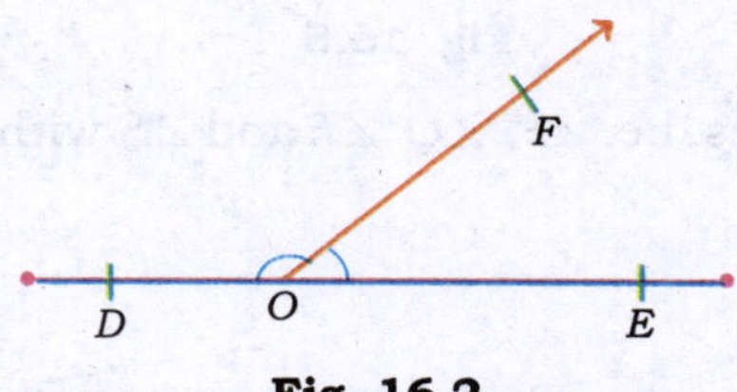

Fig. 16.2

In Fig 16.2, $\angle DOF + \angle EOF = 180°$

If the sum of two adjacent angles is 180°, then the non-common arms of the angles form a straight line. The two axioms given above together are called the **linear pair axiom**.

3. If the side QR of ΔPQR is produced to S, then $\angle PRS$ is called an exterior angle of ΔPQR at R, while $\angle QPR$ and $\angle PQR$ are called its **interior opposite angles**. (see Fig. 16.3)

4. A quadrilateral *DEFG* is called a **cyclic quadrilateral**, if all the four vertices *D, E, F* and *G* are concyclic, i.e. *D, E, F* and *G* lie on a circle.

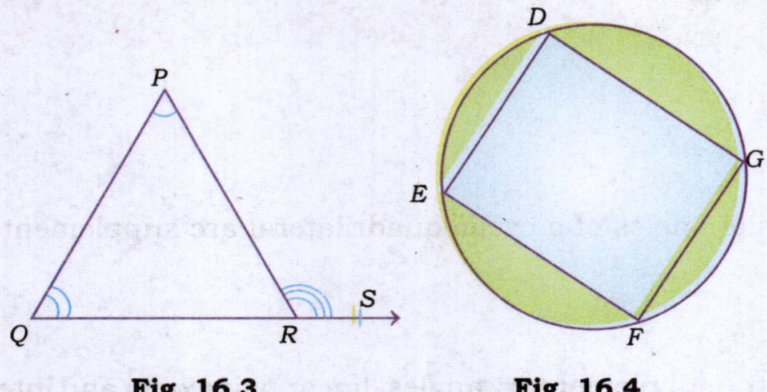

Fig. 16.3 **Fig. 16.4**

In Fig. 16.4, *DEFG* is a cyclic quadrilateral. The sum of opposite angles of a cyclic quadrilateral is always 180°, i.e. they are supplementary.

Procedure

1. Take a cardboard of suitable size and paste a white paper on it.
2. Draw a circle of suitable radius on drawing sheet.
3. Cut out the circle and paste it on white sheet on the cardboard.
4. In the circle, draw a quadrilateral *PQRS* such that all the four vertices of quadrilateral lie on the circle. Name the angles as $\angle P$, $\angle Q$, $\angle R$ and $\angle S$. (see Fig. 16.5)

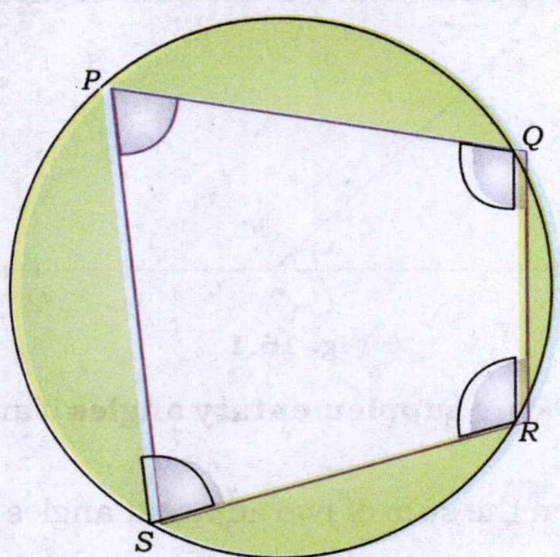

Fig. 16.5

5. Make the cut outs of the angles, i.e. $\angle P$, $\angle Q$, $\angle R$ and $\angle S$ with the help of a transparent sheet. (see Fig. 16.6)

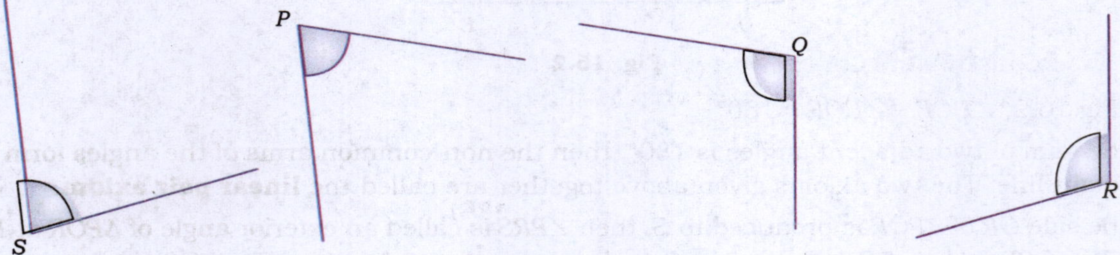

Fig. 16.6

6. By using adhesive, paste the cut outs of the opposite angles $\angle P$ and $\angle R$, $\angle Q$ and $\angle S$. (see Fig. 16.7)

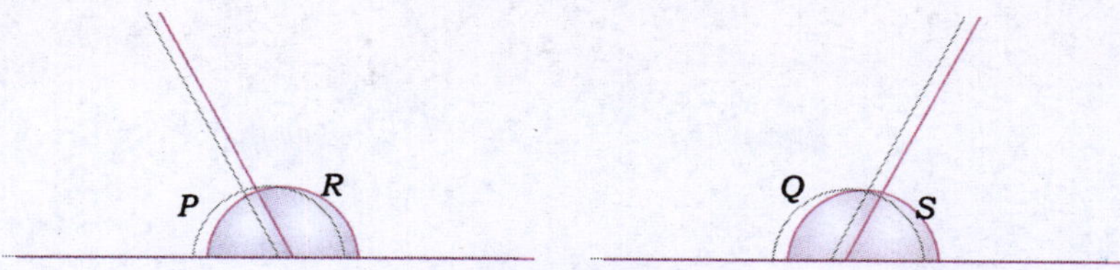

Fig. 16.7

Observation

Joining the opposite angles $\angle P$ and $\angle R$, $\angle Q$ and $\angle S$, we get straight angles. (see Fig. 16.7)
Hence, $\angle P + \angle R = 180°$ and $\angle Q + \angle S = 180°$.
By actual measurement, we have

$\angle P$ = ..., $\angle Q$ = ..., $\angle R$ = ..., $\angle S$ = ...,

So, $\angle P + \angle R$ = ..., $\angle Q + \angle S$ = ...

Hence, sum of each pair of the opposite angles of a cyclic quadrilateral is ....

Result

We have verified that the opposite angles of a cyclic quadrilateral are always supplementary.

Application

This property can be used in solving various problems in geometry.

Viva-Voce

Q.1 Define the term cyclic quadrilateral?
Ans A quadrilateral having all the vertices on the circumference of a circle is called a cyclic quadrilateral.

Q.2 What is the sum of each pair of opposite angles of a cyclic quadrilateral?
Ans 180°

Q.3 If one of the angles of a cyclic quadrilateral is 40°, then what will be the value of its opposite angle?
Ans 140°

Q.4 If the opposite sides of cyclic quadrilateral are parallel, then what is it called?
Ans Cyclic rectangle

Q.5 Is it correct that the sum of adjacent angles of a cyclic quadrilateral is 180°?
Ans No, only the sum of opposite angles of a cyclic quadrilateral is 180°.

Q.6 If one side of a cyclic quadrilateral is produced, then the exterior angle is equal to what?
Ans Sum of interior opposite angles

Q.7 Which quadrilateral is formed by the internal angle bisectors of cyclic quadrilateral?
Ans Cyclic quadrilateral

Q.8 Which property is required in a trapezium for making it a cyclic quadrilateral?
Ans Non-parallel sides of a trapezium should be equal.

Activity 17

OBJECTIVE

To form a cone from a sector of a circle and to find the formula for its curved surface area.

Prior Knowledge

1. Concept of a circle.
2. Concept of sector of a circle.
3. Concept of a cone.

Materials Required

1. Acrylic sheets
2. Adhesive tape
3. A pair of scissors
4. Geometry box
5. Marker

Theory

1. For concept of a circle refer to Activity 14.
2. **Sector of a Circle** The region between an arc and the two radii joining the centre to the end points of the arc is called a sector.

   Sectors are of two types—**minor sector** and **major sector**. Minor sector is the sector of circle, which is less than a semi-circle and major sector is the sector of circle, which is greater than a semi-circle. (see Fig. 17.1)

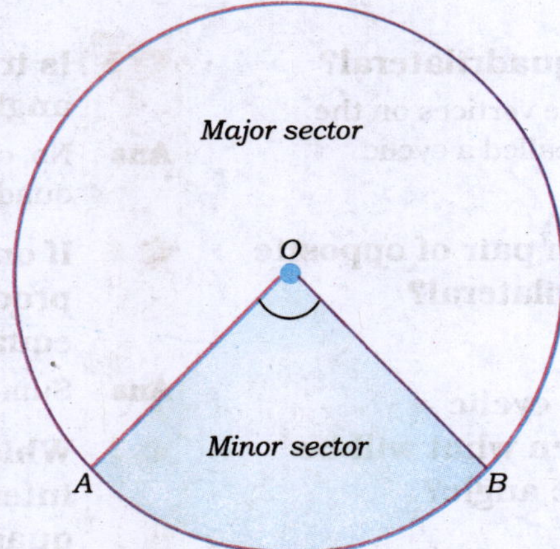

Fig. 17.1

$$\text{Area of sector} = \frac{\text{Arc length}}{\text{Circumference of circle}} \times \text{Area of the circle}$$

or $\text{Area of sector} = \dfrac{\theta°}{360°} \times$ Area of circle, where $\theta°$ is the angle between centre and radius.

3. **Cone** A right circular cone is a solid generated by revolving a line segment which passes through a fixed point and which makes a constant angle with a fixed line.

In other words, if a right angled triangle is revolved about one of the two sides forming a right angle, keeping the other sides fixed in position, then the solid so obtained by revolving the line segments is called a **right circular cone**.

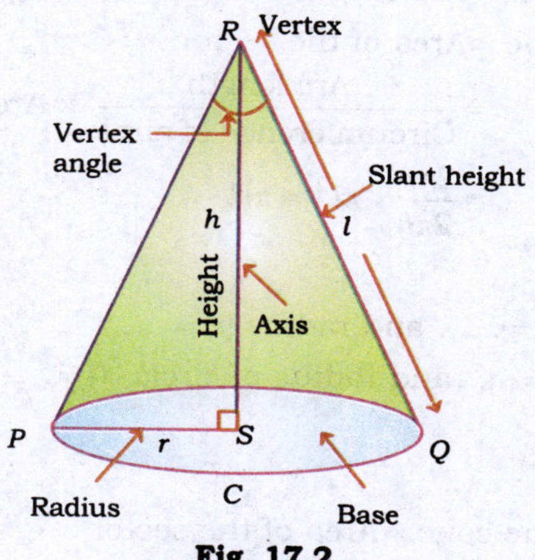

Fig. 17.2

In Fig. 17.2, a right angled ΔPSR on revolving about the segment *RS*, generates a right circular cone in which *PQC* is a circle.

Procedure

1. From acrylic sheet, cut out a circle of radius *l*. (see Fig. 17.3)
2. Now, cut out a sector having angle $\theta°$ from the circle. (see Fig. 17.4)

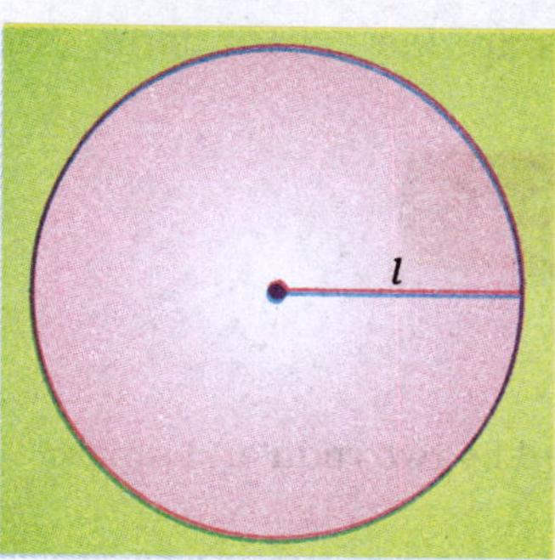

Fig. 17.3

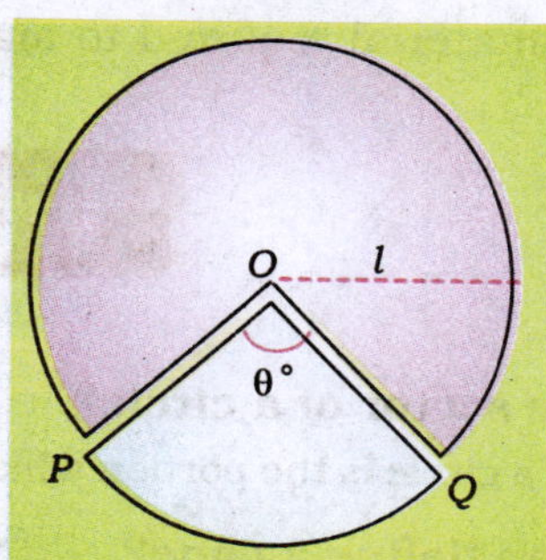

Fig. 17.4

3. To form a cone, bring together both the radii of the sector and by using a adhesive tape, attach the ends. (see Fig. 17.5)

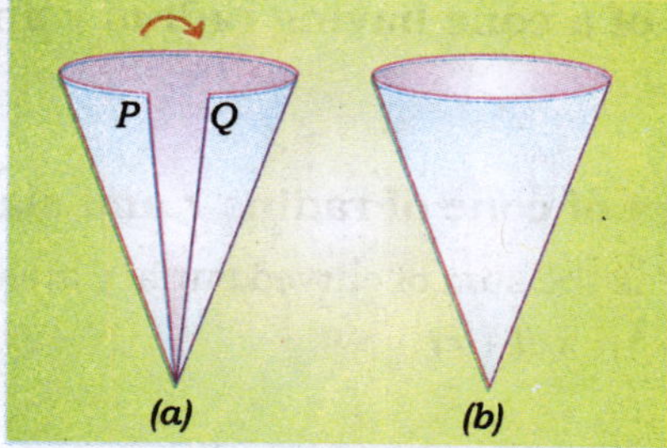

Fig. 17.5

Observation

From the Fig. 17.5, we have

Radius of the base of cone = r

Slant height of the cone = Radius of circle = l

Circumference of the base of cone = Arc length of sector = $2\pi r$

Now, curved surface area of cone = Area of the sector

$$= \frac{\text{Arc length}}{\text{Circumference of circle}} \times \text{Area of the circle}$$

$$= \frac{2\pi r}{2\pi l} \times \pi l^2 = \pi r l$$

By actual measurement,

The slant height (l) of the cone = ... and radius (r) = ...

$\theta°$ = ... and radius of circle (l) = ...

So, Area of the sector = ...,

curved surface area of the cone = ...

Hence, curved surface area of the cone = Area of the sector

Result

We have derived the formula for calculating the curved surface area of cone.

Applications

This result is useful in

1. estimation of canvas required to make a conical tent.
2. estimation of material required to make joker's cap, ice-cream cone, etc.

Q.1 What is the sector of a circle?

Ans The sector of a circle is the portion which is enclosed by two radii and an arc.

Q.2 How will you define a cone?

Ans A cone is a three dimensional geometrical shape that has one circular base and one vertex.

Q.3 What is the the curved surface area of a cone of radius r and slant height l?

Ans Curved surface area of a cone = $\pi r l$

Q.4 What is the slant height of a cone having radius r and height h?

Ans Slant height, $l = \sqrt{h^2 + r^2}$

Q.5 What is total surface area of cone of radius r and slant height l?

Ans The total surface area of cone is the sum of curved surface area and area of base.

$\therefore$ Total surface area = $\pi r l + \pi r^2 = \pi r(l + r)$

Activity 18

OBJECTIVE

To find the relationship among the volumes of a right circular cone and a hemisphere of equal radii and equal heights.

Prior Knowledge

1. Concept of cone and its volume.
2. Concept of sphere, hemisphere and its volume.

Materials Required

1. Cardboard
2. Geometry box
3. Hollow ball
4. Cutter
5. Marker
6. Sand or salt
7. Adhesive
8. Acrylic sheets

Theory

1. For concept of cone refer to Activity 17. Let r be the radius and h be the height of cone.

$$\text{Volume of cone} = \frac{1}{3}\pi r^2 h \text{ cu units}$$

2. A **sphere** is three dimensional figure (solid figure) which is made up of all points in the space, which lie at a constant distance, from a fixed point called the centre of the sphere and the constant distance is called its radius. (see Fig. 18.1)

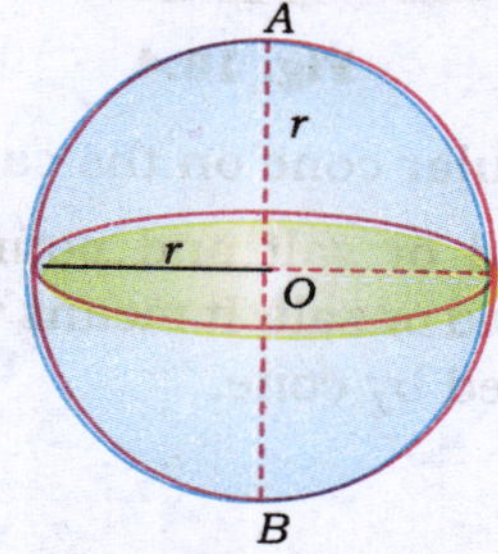

Fig. 18.1

$$\text{Volume of sphere of radius } r \text{ units} = \frac{4}{3}\pi r^3 \text{ cu units}$$

3. A plane through the centre of a sphere divides the sphere into two equal parts, each of which is called a **hemisphere**. (see Fig. 18.2)

$$\text{Volume of hemisphere of radius } r \text{ units} = \frac{2}{3}\pi r^3 \text{ cu units}$$

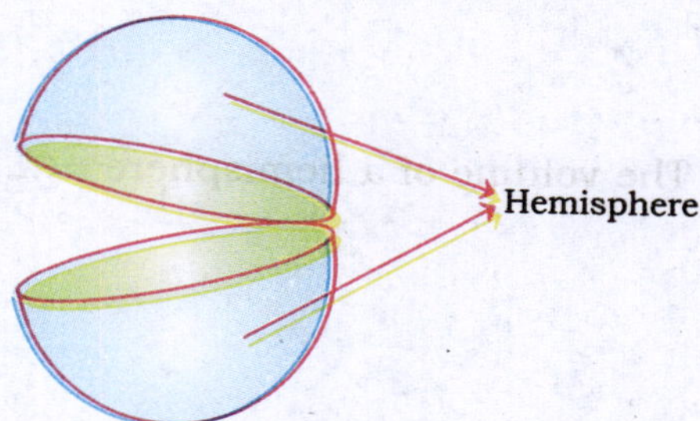

Fig. 18.2

Procedure

1. Take a hollow ball having radius a units (say $a = 4$ cm) and cut it into two halves. (see Fig. 18.3)

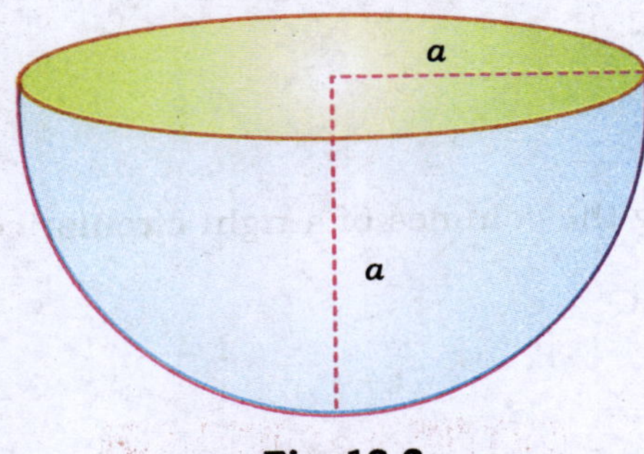

Fig. 18.3

2. Take an acrylic sheet and cut it to get right circular cone of radius a units and height a units. (see Fig. 18.4)

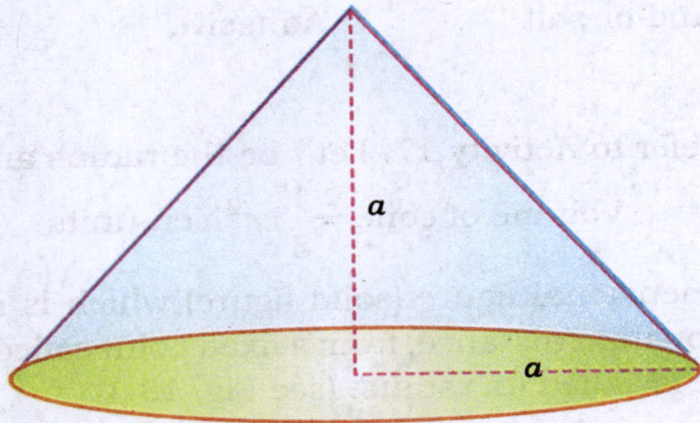

Fig. 18.4

3. Place hemisphere and right circular cone on the cardboard.
4. Let the cone be filled with sand or salt and pour it twice into the hemisphere. Then, hemisphere is fully filled with sand or salt. It means that hemisphere contains double of the amount of sand/salt as contained by cone.

Observations

It is concluded from point 4 of procedure that volume of cone $= \frac{1}{2}$ volume of hemisphere.

Hence, volume of cone : volume of hemisphere = 1: 2

By actual measurement,
The radius of cone = The height of cone = ...
The volume of a cone ......
The volume of a hemisphere ......
Hence, the volume of a cone : The volume of a hemisphere = ...

Result

We have got the relationship among the volumes of a right circular cone and a hemisphere of equal radii and equal heights.

Applications

This activity may be used in

1. deriving the formula for volume of a cone and that of a hemisphere from the formula of volume of a cylinder.
2. making packages of the similar material in containers of different shapes such as hemisphere, cone, etc.

Q.1 **What is the formula for the volume of a right circular cone having height *h* and radius *r*?**

Ans $\frac{1}{3}\pi r^2 h$

Q.2 **What is the formula for the volume of a hemisphere of radius *r*?**

Ans $\frac{2}{3}\pi r^3$

Q.3 **'If the radius of cone is halved and height is doubled, then the volume will be doubled'. Is it possible?**

Ans No, the volume will become half.

Q.4 **What is the relationship among the volumes of a right circular cone and a hemisphere of equal radii and equal heights?**

Ans 1 : 2

Q.5 **What is the volume of a sphere having radius *r*?**

Ans $\frac{4}{3}\pi r^3$

Activity 19

OBJECTIVE

To obtain the formula for the surface area of a sphere.

Prior Knowledge

1. Basic knowledge about shape of a sphere.
2. Basic concept of a circle and its area.

Materials Required

1. Cardboard/Wooden strips
2. Thick sheet of paper
3. Geometry box
4. String
5. Measuring tape
6. Adhesive
7. A ball
8. A pair of scissors/Cutter
9. A pin

Theory

1. A **sphere** is three dimensional figure (solid figure) which is made up of all points in the space, which lie at constant distance, from a fixed point called the centre of the sphere and the constant distance is called its **radius**. (see Fig. 19.1)

   A line segment through the centre of a sphere and with the end points on the sphere is called a **diameter** of the sphere. (see Fig. 19.1)

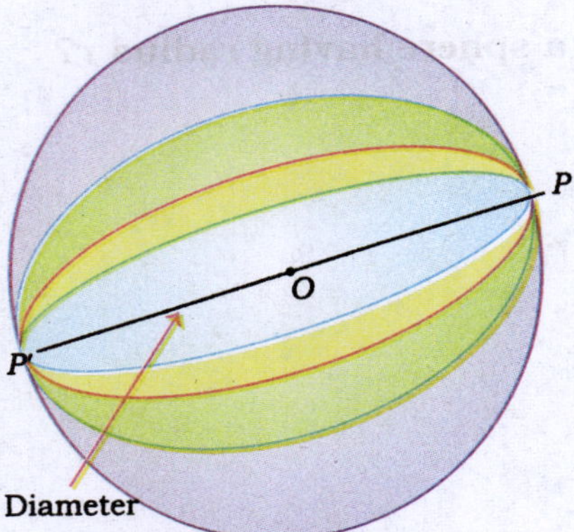

Fig. 19.1

2. For concept of circle refer to Activity 14.

   Area of a circle = πr^2

Procedure

1. Take a spherical ball and by placing it between two vertical boards or wooden strips, find its diameter (d). The radius of sphere, r will be half of diameter. (see Fig. 19.2)

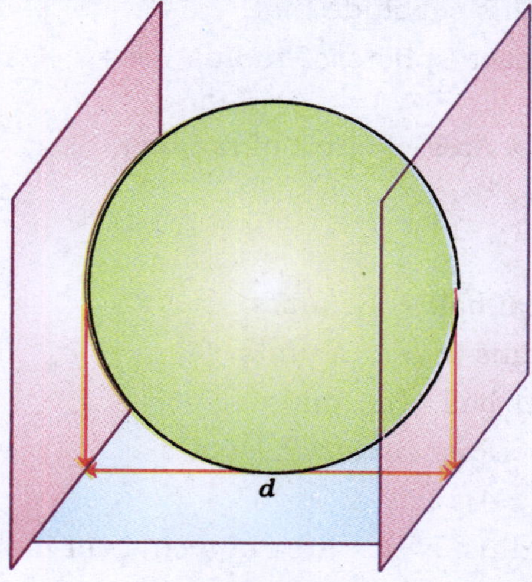

Fig. 19.2

2. Mark the topmost part of ball and fix a pin. (see Fig. 19.3)
3. Wrap the ball (spirally) with string completely, by taking support of pin such that no space is left uncovered. (see Fig. 19.3)

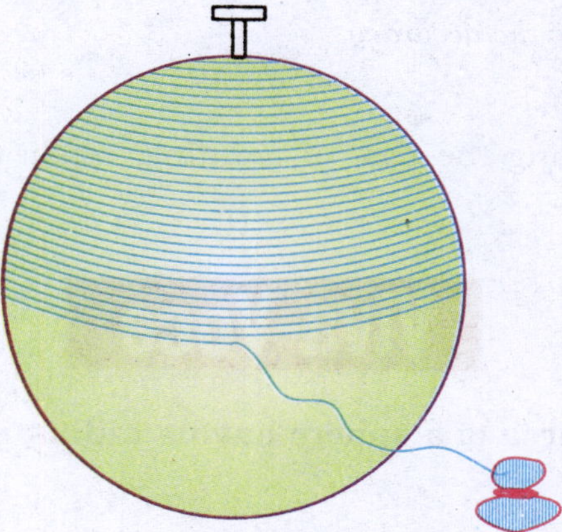

Fig. 19.3

4. Mark the starting and ending points on the string (for accuracy, it should be thinner) measure the length between these two marks and denoted by l.
5. Now, unwind the string from the ball.
6. Draw four circles on the thick sheet of paper with radius equal to the radius of the ball, i.e. r.
7. Now, fill the circles one-by-one with string which wound around the ball. (see Fig. 19.4)

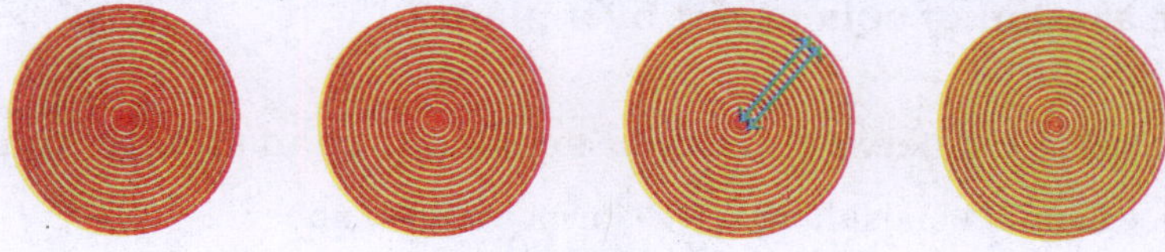

Fig. 19.4

Observation

Let the length of string which covers a circle (radius r) is denoted by x.

The string which had completely covered the surface area of the ball, has been used completely to fill the region of four circles. This conclude that

Length of string needed to cover sphere of radius $r = 4 \times$ (Length of string needed to cover one circle)

i.e. Surface area of sphere $= 4 \times$ Area of circle of radius r

$\therefore$ Surface area of sphere $= 4\pi r^2$

By actual measurement,

Diameter (d) of the spherical ball = ... units

Radius (r) = ... units

Length of string l used to cover ball = ... units

Length of string x used to cover one circle = ... units

So, $l = 4 \times$ ......

Surface area of a sphere of radius, $r = 4 \times$ Area of a circle of radius, $r = 4\pi r^2$.

Result

We have verified the formula for the surface area of sphere experimentally.

Note *1. Measure the diameter of ball carefully.*

2. Wrap the ball completely so that no space is left uncovered.

3. Thinner the string more is the accuracy.

Application

This activity is useful in finding the cost of painting, repairing, constructing spherical and hemispherical objects.

Viva-Voce

Q.1 What is the surface area of a sphere having radius r units?

Ans $4\pi r^2$

Q.2 What is a hemisphere?

Ans The equal half part of sphere is called a hemisphere.

Q.3 Is sphere a two dimensional figure?

Ans No, sphere is a three dimensional figure.

Q.4 Are the total surface area and curved surface area of a sphere equal?

Ans Yes

Q.5 What is the section of sphere cut by a plane?

Ans Circle

Q.6 What is the relation between curved surface area of sphere and hemisphere?

Ans Curved surface area of hemisphere $= \frac{1}{2} \times$ (surface area of sphere)

Q.7 What is the total surface area of hemisphere?

Ans Total surface area = curved surface area + area of circular section $= (2\pi r^2) + \pi r^2 = 3\pi r^2$

Activity 20

OBJECTIVE

To draw histograms for classes of equal widths and varying widths.

Prior Knowledge

1. Knowledge about collection of data.
2. Concept of histogram.

Materials Required

1. Graph paper
2. Geometry box
3. Adhesive
4. Sketch pens
5. A pair of scissors
6. A piece of cardboard

Theory

1. **Collection of Data**

   The facts or figures which are numerical or otherwise, collected with a definite purpose (i.e. observation/information collected), are called data. Some basic terms related to data are given below:

   (i) The data collected by the investigator himself for a definite plan or purpose is known as **primary data**.

   (ii) The data collected by someone and used by any other person is known as **secondary data**.

   (iii) The data obtained in original form is called **raw data** or **ungrouped data**.

   (iv) The data condensed into classes or groups such as presentation is known as **grouped data**.

2. **Histogram** A histogram is the graphical representation of a grouped frequency distribution with continuous classes in the form of rectangles with class intervals as bases and the corresponding frequencies as heights. There being no gap between any two consecutive rectangles.

   Histogram is commonly used to show frequency distribution.

Procedure

1. First, collect the data from daily life such as weights/heights of children in a class, then make a frequency distribution table.

   Case I For classes of equal widths,

Class	$x_1 - x_2$	$x_2 - x_3$	$x_3 - x_4$	$x_4 - x_5$	$x_5 - x_6$
Frequency	f_1	f_2	f_3	f_4	f_5

Case II For classes of varying widths,

Here, $$x_4 - x_6 = 2(x_1 - x_2)$$

Class	$x_1 - x_2$ (width d)	$x_2 - x_3$ (width d)	$x_3 - x_4$ (width d)	$x_4 - x_6$ (width $2d$)
Frequency	f_1	f_2	f_3	f_4
Modified frequency	f_1	f_2	f_3	$F' = f_4/2$

2. Take two graph papers and paste it on a piece of cardboard sheet.
3. Now, draw two perpendicular axes $X'OX$ and YOY' on each graph paper. (see Fig. 20.1)
4. At equal distances, mark classes on X-axis and frequency on Y-axis. (see Fig. 20.1)

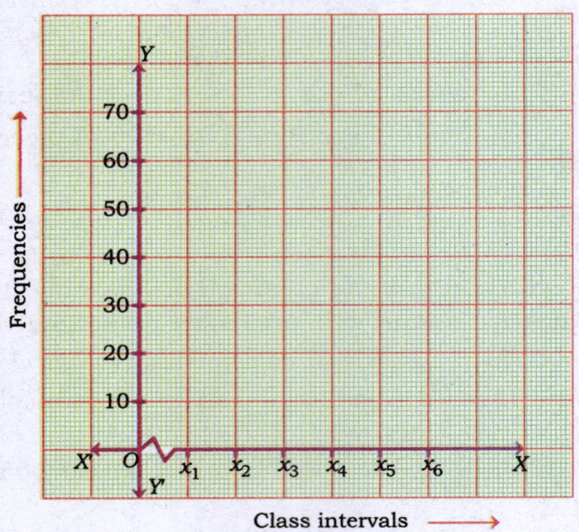

Fig. 20.1

5. On one graph paper, draw rectangles of equal widths and heights f_1, f_2, f_3, f_4 and f_5 on intervals $(x_1 - x_2)$, $(x_2 - x_3)$, $(x_3 - x_4)$, $(x_4 - x_5)$ and $(x_5 - x_6)$ respectively. (see Fig. 20.2)

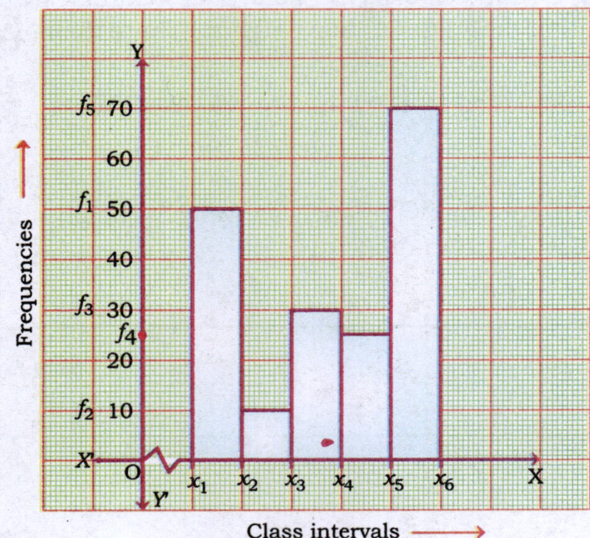

Fig. 20.2

6. On another graph paper, draw rectangles of heights f_1, f_2, f_3 and F' on intervals $(x_1 - x_2)$, $(x_2 - x_3)$, $(x_3 - x_4)$ and $(x_4 - x_6)$ respectively. (see Fig. 20.3)

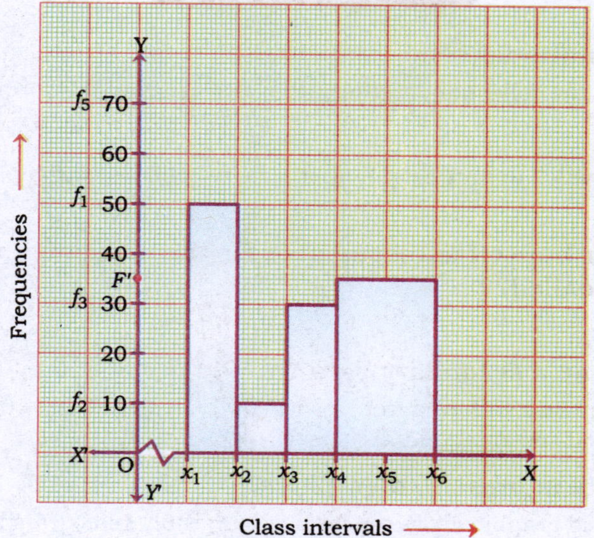

Fig. 20.3

Observations

1. Different numerical values can be taken for x_1, x_2, x_3, x_4, x_5 and x_6.
2. With these numerical values, histograms of equal width and varying width can be drawn.

Case I For the classes of equal widths,

1. The intervals are

   $x_1 - x_2 = \ldots\ldots\ldots$, $x_2 - x_3 = \ldots\ldots\ldots$, $x_3 - x_4 = \ldots\ldots\ldots$,

   $x_4 - x_5 = \ldots\ldots\ldots$, $x_5 - x_6 = \ldots\ldots\ldots$

2. $f_1 = \ldots\ldots\ldots$, $f_2 = \ldots\ldots\ldots$, $f_3 = \ldots\ldots\ldots$,

   $f_4 = \ldots\ldots\ldots$, $f_5 = \ldots\ldots\ldots$

Case II For the classes of varying widths,

1. The intervals are

   $x_1 - x_2 = \ldots\ldots\ldots$, $x_2 - x_3 = \ldots\ldots\ldots$,

   $x_3 - x_4 = \ldots\ldots\ldots$, $x_4 - x_6 = \ldots\ldots\ldots$

2. $f_1 = \ldots\ldots\ldots$, $f_2 = \ldots\ldots\ldots$, $f_3 = \ldots\ldots\ldots$,

   $f_4 = \ldots\ldots\ldots$, $F' = \dfrac{f_4}{2} = \ldots\ldots\ldots$

Result

We have drawn histogram of equal widths and varying widths by using the collected data.

Application

Histograms can be used pictorially in representing large data in a concise form.

Viva-Voce

Q.1 Define the term statistics?

Ans Statistics deals with the collection, organisation, analysis and interpretation of data.

Q.2 What is data?

Ans The facts or figures which are numerical or otherwise collected with a definite purpose are called data.

Q.3 If the investigator himself is responsible for the collection of data, then what is this type of data called?

Ans Primary

Q.4 How will you define a secondary data?

Ans When the information was gathered from a source which already had the information stored, the data obtained is called secondary data.

Q.5 In what form, data is presented graphically?

Ans Data can be presented graphically in the form of bar graph, histogram and frequency polygons.

Q.6 What is a histogram?

Ans A histogram is the graphical representation of a grouped frequency distribution with continuous classes in the form of rectangles with class intervals as bases and the corresponding frequencies as heights.

Q.7 What do you understand by grouped data?

Ans Grouped data is a statistical term used in a data analysis. A raw data can be organised by constructing a table showing the frequency distribution of the variable (whose values are given in the raw data). Such a frequency table is often reffered to as grouped data.

Q.8 The data collected by a student regarding maximum and minimum temperature of a city from a newspaper. This is an example of which data?

Ans Secondary data

Q.10 What is the singular form of data?

Ans Datum

Projects

Project 1

OBJECTIVE

Story of π

Prior Knowledge

1. Irrational numbers
2. Concept of π (pi)
3. Area of circle and square

Theory

1. (i) Irrational numbers are those numbers which cannot be expressed in the form of $\frac{p}{q}$, where p, q are integers and $q \neq 0$. e.g. $\sqrt{2}$, $\sqrt{3}$, $\sqrt{5}$, $\sqrt{7}$, etc.

   (ii) Also, irrational numbers are those numbers whose decimal expansions are non-terminating non-recurring.

2. (i) The number π (pi) is an irrational number, which means that its value cannot be expressed in the form of $\frac{p}{q}$, where p, q are integers and $q \neq 0$.

   (ii) It is also a transcendental number.

   (iii) The constant π is the first Greek letter, which is used to find the circumference or perimeter of a circle.

   (iv) The number π is the ratio of the circumference of a circle to its diameter. i.e. $\pi = c/d$, where c is the circumference of a circle and d is the diameter of a circle.

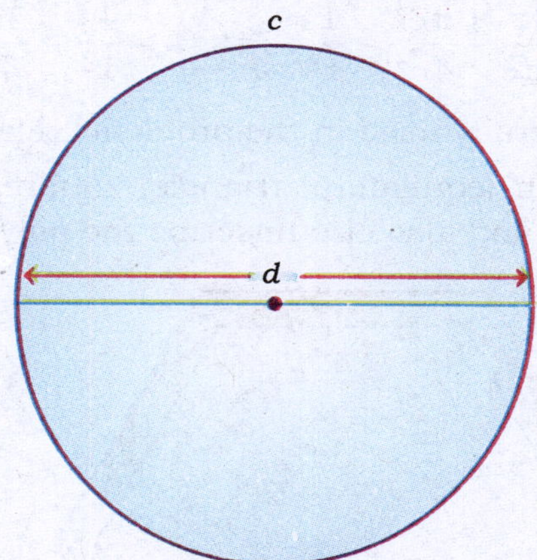

   (v) The first scientist Archimedes Syracure (287 BC) gave the first theoretical calculated value of pi (π).

3. (i) Area of circle $= \pi r^2 = \frac{\pi d^2}{4}$, where r and d are the radius and diameter of circle, respectively and $r = \frac{d}{2}$.

   (ii) Area of square = Side × Side

HISTORY of π (pi)

Different mathematicians calculated value of π in different manners, some of them are given below.

1. Ahmes in Rhind Papyrus

Ahmes states that, if a square is drawn with a side whose length is $\frac{8}{9}$th of the diameter of a circle, then the area of the square so formed and area of the circle would be same.

Area of circle $= \pi\left(\frac{d}{2}\right)^2 = \frac{\pi d^2}{4}$ and Area of square $= \left(\frac{8}{9}d\right)^2 = \frac{64}{81}d^2$

According to the above statement, $\frac{\pi d^2}{4} = \frac{64}{81}d^2$

$\Rightarrow \quad \pi = \frac{64 \times 4}{81} \Rightarrow \pi = \frac{256}{81} = 3.16049382716049382 71$

2. Archimedes

(i) The ratio of the area of a circle to that of a square with side equal to the circle's diameter is close to 11 : 14.

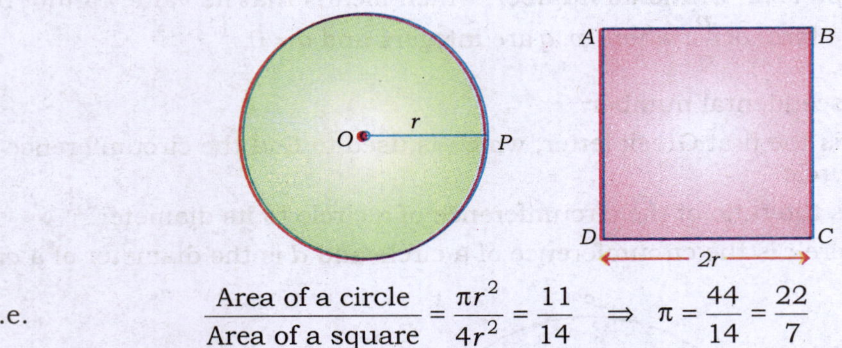

i.e. $\frac{\text{Area of a circle}}{\text{Area of a square}} = \frac{\pi r^2}{4r^2} = \frac{11}{14} \Rightarrow \pi = \frac{44}{14} = \frac{22}{7}$

This approximate value is generally used in the problems related to mensuration.

(ii) He inscribed a regular polygon (equilateral triangle, square, regular pentagon, regular hexagon, etc.) in a given circle and also circumscribe the polygon about the same circle.

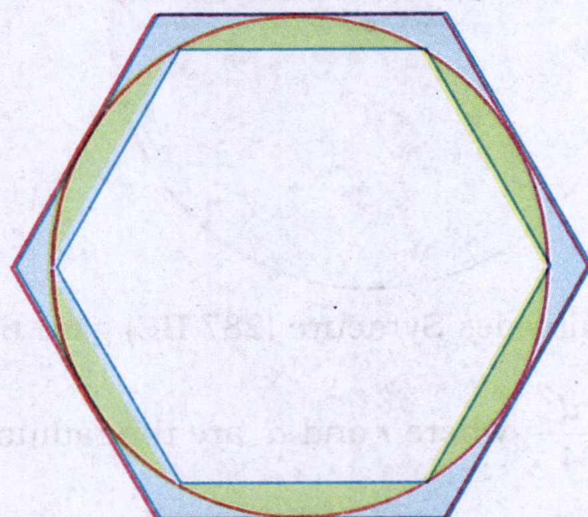

In both the cases, the perimeter of the polygon gets closer to the circumference of the circle. This process is also repeated with 12, 24, 48, etc., sided regular polygon.

In each time, perimeter is closer to the circumference of the circle.

He finally concludes that π is more than $3\frac{10}{71}$ but less than $3\frac{1}{7}$.

i.e. $$3\frac{10}{71} < \pi < 3\frac{1}{7}$$

or $$3.\overline{14084507042253521126760563380281690} < \pi < 3.\overline{142857}$$

3. **Liu Hui** (Chinese mathematician) Liu Hui used regular polygon with increasing number of sides to approximate the circle. He used only inscribed circles while Archimedes used both inscribed and circumscribed circles. Liu's approximation of π was

$$\frac{3927}{1250} = 3.1416$$

4. **Zu Chongzhi** (Chinese astronomer and mathematician)

He found the value of $\pi = \frac{355}{113}$

$$= 3.\overline{1415929203539823008849557522123893805309734513274336283185840707964601769911504424778761061946902654867256637168}$$

5. **John Wallis** (Professor of Mathematics at Cambridge and Oxford Universities)

He gave the following formula for π

$$\frac{\pi}{2} = \frac{2\times 2}{1\times 3} \times \frac{4\times 4}{3\times 5} \times \frac{6\times 6}{5\times 7} \times \ldots \times \frac{2n \times 2n}{(2n-1)(2n+1)}$$

6. **Brouncker** He obtained the following value of $\frac{4}{\pi}$.

$$\frac{4}{\pi} = 1 + \cfrac{1^2}{2 + \cfrac{3^2}{2 + \cfrac{5^2}{2 + \cfrac{7^2}{2 + \cfrac{9^2}{2+\ldots}}}}}$$

7. **Aryabhata** He gave the value of π as $\frac{62832}{20000} = 3.14156$

8. **Brahmagupta** He gave the value of π as $\sqrt{10} = 3.162277$

9. **Al-Khwarizmi** He gave the value of π as 3.1416.

10. **Babylonian** He used the value of π as $3 + \frac{1}{8} = 3.125$.

11. **Yasumasa** Kanada and his team at University of Tokyo, calculated the value of π to 1.24 trillion decimal places.

12. **Francois** Viete calculated π correct to nine decimal places. He calculated the value of π to be between the numbers 15926535 and 3.1415926537.

13. **S. Ramanujan** calculated the value of π as $\sqrt[4]{9^2 + \frac{19^2}{22}} =$ 2652..., which is correct to eight decimal places.

14. **Leonhard Euler** came up with an interesting expression for obtaining the value of π as

$$\frac{2}{\pi} = \left(1-\frac{1}{4}\right)\left(1-\frac{1}{16}\right)\left(1-\frac{1}{36}\right)\left(1-\frac{1}{64}\right)\left(1-\frac{1}{100}\right)\ldots,$$

Paradox of a π (pi)

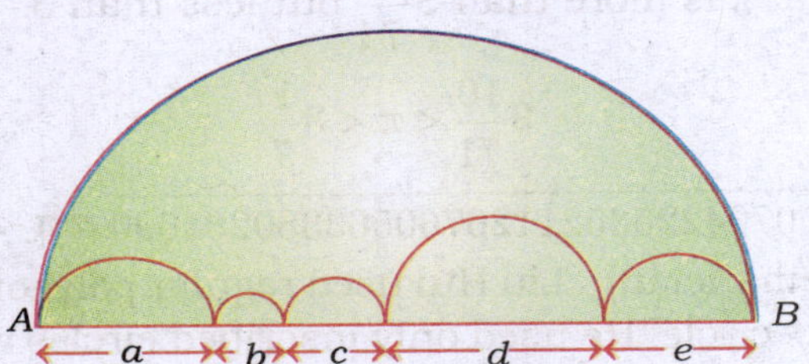

In the above figure, perimeter of the semi-circle with diameter $AB = \frac{\pi}{2}(AB)$

∴ Sum of the perimeters of smaller semi-circles

$$= \frac{\pi a}{2} + \frac{\pi b}{2} + \frac{\pi c}{2} + \frac{\pi d}{2} + \frac{\pi e}{2} = \frac{\pi}{2}(a + b + c + d + e)$$

This may not appear to be true but it is. Let us now proceed in the following way. Increase the number of smaller semi-circles along the fixed line segment AB say of 4 units.

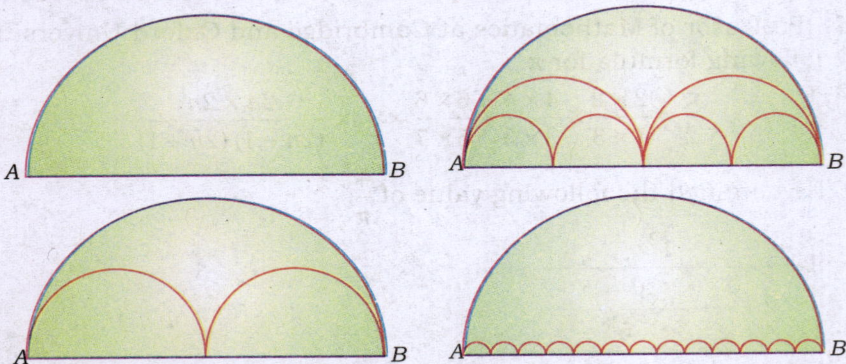

In the above figures, the sum of the lengths of the perimeters of smaller semi-circles appears to be approaching the length of the diameter AB but infact it is not, because the lengths of the perimeters of the smaller semi-circles is $\frac{\pi \times 4}{2} = 2\pi$, while length of AB is 4 units. So, both cannot be the same.

Learning Outcomes

Here, we conclude that generally the value of π is used as $\frac{22}{7}$ or 3.141 in different areas of field.

Application

The value of π is used in finding areas and perimeters of designs related to circles and sector of circles. It has applications in the construction of racetracks and engineering equipments.

Project 2

OBJECTIVE

Chronology of Indian Mathematicians with their contributions.

List of Famous Indian Mathematicians

1. Aryabhata (476-550 AD)
2. Brahmagupta (598-668 AD)
3. Bhaskaracharya (1114-1185 AD)
4. Srinivasa Ramanujan (1887-1920 AD)

ARYABHATA [476-550 AD]

Life History

Aryabhata has said in his creation Aryabhattiya that he was 23 yr old, when he wrote Aryabhattiya and upto that time, 3600 years of Kaliyug had elapsed. This works out that he wrote the manuscript in 499 AD and his year of birth was 476 AD.

Aryabhata has also said in the manuscript that he has given the knowledge attained at Kusumpur (Pataliputra) while studying. This gives the impression that he was born at Pataliputra but according to the views of majority, he was born in South India (in Ashmak district, which is on the bank of river Godavari).

The world famous historian mathematician Dr Bhou-Daji of Maharashtra traced the manuscript of Aryabhattiya in 1864 from South India and published its contents.

Aryabhattiya is in Sanskrit and is divided in four major parts called 'Pads'. The manuscript contains a total of 153 Shlokas and their distribution is given below :

1. **Dashgeetika** pad containing 33 shlokas.
2. **Ganitpad** containing 25 shlokas.
3. **Kalkriya** pad containing 25 shlokas.
4. **Goladhyay** containing 50 shlokas.

His Contributions

In Mathematics Field

1. Aryabhata created a new method of enumerating numbers using Sanskrit alphabets. According to this, he gave the following numerical values to 25 consonants.

   क : 1, ख : 2, ग : 3, घ : 4, ङ : 5, च : 6, छ : 7,ज : 8, झ : 9, ञ : 10, ट : 11, ठ : 12, ड : 13, ढ : 14, ण : 15, त : 16, थ : 17, द : 18, ध :19, न : 20, प : 21, फ : 22, ब : 23, भ : 24, म : 25, य : 30, र : 40, ल : 50, व : 60, श : 70, ष : 80, स : 90, ह :100

He gave the following values to vowels.

अ : 1, ई : 100, ऊ :10000, ऋ :1000000, लृ: 100000000, ए :10000000000, ऐ :1000000000000, ओ :100000000000000, औ : 10000000000000000

As an example, Aryabhata says that in a Mahayug, the earth revolves around the sun 4320000 times. According to the above numerical system, Aryabhat has stated it as

ख्: $2 \times 10000 = 20000$

यु: $30 \times 10000 = 300000$

घृ: $4 \times 1000000 = 4000000$

खुयुघृ $= 4320000$

2. Aryabhata has summarised important principles of arithmetic, geometry and algebra in 33 shlokas of Ganitpad only. In these shlokas, he has given formulae for finding:
   - squares and square roots.
   - cubes and cube roots.
   - area of squares, triangles and circles.
   - volume of a sphere.

   His most important contribution was the value of π. The ratio between the circumference and the diameter of a circle upto four places of decimals is 3.1416. He stated that it is the approximate value of π. He was the first Indian mathematician who has stated that it is the approximate value of π.
3. Aryabhata has given methods of drawing a circle, a triangle and quadrilateral and solving of quadratic equations.
4. He has stated and verified Pythagoras theorem through examples.
5. Another important contribution of Aryabhata has been formation of tables of sine and cosine functions at intervals of 3°45′ each.
6. Aryabhata has also written about astronomy and astrology in his Goladhyay. He was the first mathematician who declared that the earth revolves about its axis and the Nakshtras are still, which was against the mythological statements. He also described about solar and lunar eclipses and reasons for their occurring.

In Astronomy Field

1. Aryabhata also did a considerable amount of work in astronomy. He knew that the earth is rotating on an axis around the sun and the moon rotated around it.
2. He also discovered the position of nine planets and stated that these also revolved around the sun. He pointed out the eclipses; both lunar and solar.
3. Aryabhata stated the correct number of days in a year that is 365.
4. He was the first person to mention that the earth was not flat but in fact a spherical shape.
5. He also gave the circumference and diameter of the earth and the radius of the orbits of 9 planets.

Death

This great mathematician died in 550 BC. He was one of the first in the line of great mathematicians in Indian history. His contributions to mathematics and science plays major role in solving many problems.

BRAHMAGUPTA [598-668 AD]

Life History

Brahmagupta was an Indian mathematician and astronomer belonging to classical age. On the basis of theoretical treatises, the 'Brahmasphuta-Siddhanta' (extensive treatise of Brahma) and 'The Khandakhadyaka', it gather that he was born 598 AD in Bhillamala (modern Bhinmal), a city in the state of Rajasthan of present-day North-West India. His father was Jisnugupta. His likely lived most of his life in Bhillamala during the reign of king Vyaghramukha. As a result, Brahmagupta is often referred to as Bhillamalacharya, that is the teacher from Bhillamala. He was the head of the Astronomical observatory at Ujjain and during those period, he wrote his two surviving treatises, both on mathematics and astronomy.

His Contributions

In Mathematics Field

1. He was first man who used zero as a number. He gave rules to compute with zero.
2. He gave four methods of multiplication which are given as:
   (i) a positive number multiplied by a positive number, which is positive.
   (ii) a positive number multiplied by a negative number, which is negative.
   (iii) a negative number multiplied by a positive number, which is negative.
   (iv) a negative number multiplied by a negative number, which is positive.
3. He gave the formula, which is used in GP, i.e.
$$a + ar + ar^2 + ar^3 + \dots + ar^{n-1} = \frac{a(r^n - 1)}{r - 1};\ r > 1$$
4. He gave the following formulae related to cyclic quadrilateral, which is famously known as Brahmagupta's formula.
   (i) Area of cyclic quadrilateral with sides $a, b, c, d = \sqrt{(s-a)(s-b)(s-c)(s-d)}$
   where, $2s = a + b + c + d$
   (ii) Length of its diagonals $= \sqrt{\frac{bc + ad}{ab + cd}(ac + bd)}, \sqrt{\frac{ab + cd}{bc + ad}(ac + bd)}$

In Astronomy Field

1. His contribution in astronomy can be understood by the statement of 'Edward **Sachau**' that "Brahmagupta, it was he who taught Arabs astronomy."
2. In the chapter seven of his Brahmasphuta-Siddhanta, Brahmagupta rebuts the idea that the moon is farther from the earth than the sun, which is maintained in scriptures.
3. Some of the important contributions made by Brahmagupta in astronomy are methods for calculating the position of heavenly bodies over time (ephemerides), their rising and setting, conjunctions and the calculation of solar and lunar eclipses.

Death

This great mathematician died In 668 AD. He was one of the greatest mathematician in Indian history and his contributions to Mathematics and Science have made major differences to various mathematical problems by establishing the basic rules which help us to find their solutions. He was honored by the title given to him by a fellow scientist.
"Ganita Chakra Chudamani" which is translated as "The gem of the circle of mathematicians".

BHASKARACHARYA [1114-1185 AD]

Life History

Bhaskaracharya was also known as Bhaskara. He was one of the most powerful and creative mathematician of ancient India. He was born in 1114 AD in Bijapur in modern Karnataka.

Bhaskaracharya and his work represents a significant contribution to mathematical and astronomical knowledge in the 12th century.

He was bestowed a suitable title by Ganesh Daivadhya for his genius work in Mathematics and astronomy calling Bhaskaracharya 'Ganakachakra Chudamani' which means 'gem among all the calculators of astronomical phenomena'. He became the head of the astronomical observatory at Ujjain, the leading mathematical centre in India at that time.

His Contributions

In Mathematics Field

1. His main work was 'Siddhanta Shiromani', which was divided into four parts called Lilawati, Bijaganit, Grahaganit and Goladhyaya. These four sections deal with arithmetic, algebra, Mathematics of planets and spheres, respectively.
2. He was the first to give that any number divided by zero, gives infinity.
3. He was written a lot about zero, surds, permutation and combination.

   He wrote, "The hundredth part of the circumference of a circle seems to be straight". Our Earth is a big sphere and that's why, it appears to be flat.
4. He gave the formulae like $\sin(A \pm B) = \sin A \cos B \pm \cos A \sin B$.
5. He calculated derivatives of trigonometric functions and formulae. He also developed the spherical trigonometry along with a number of other trigonometric results.
6. He explained the solutions of quadratic, cubic and quadratic indeterminate equations.
7. He developed a proof of Pythagoras theorem by calculating the same area in two different ways and these cancel out terms to get $a^2 + b^2 = c^2$.
8. He gave the first general method for finding the solution of the Pell's equation $x^2 - xy^2 - 1$.

In Astronomy Field

1. Bhaskaracharya also did a considerable amount of work in astronomy. He found the position of planets.
2. He also found the occurrence of eclipses and cosmography.
3. In his book 'Surya Siddhant', he wrote about the gravitational force that helps to keep the planets, the sun and the moon in their respective orbits much before the world could even wake and realize these findings.
4. He accurately calculated the time that earth took to revolve around the sun as 365.2588 days i.e. a difference of 3 min of modern acceptance of 365.2563 days.

Death

This great mathematician died in 1185 AD. He was one of the great mathematician and astronomer in Indian history.

SRINIVASA RAMANUJAN [1887-1920 AD]

Life History

Srinivasa Ramanujan, an Indian mathematician was born in 22nd December, 1887 in Madras, India. He received no formal education in Mathematics but made important contribution to advancement of Mathematics. In recognition of his achievement, his birth date 22nd December is celebrated in India as Mathematics day.

His Contribution in Mathematics Field

1. Ramanujan made extraordinary contributions to mathematical analysis, number theory, infinite series and continued fractions.
2. Ramanujan demonstrated unusual mathematical skill at school, winning accolades and awards.
3. When he was 17 yr old, he had conducted his own mathematical research on Bernoulli numbers and the Euler-Mascheroni constant.
4. He discovered theorems of his own and rediscovered Euler's identity independently.
5. Ramanujan showed that any big number can be written as the sum of not more than four prime numbers. He also showed that how to divided the number into two or more squares or cubes.
6. When Mr GH Hardy came to see Ramanujan in taxi number 1729, then Ramanujan said that 1729 is smallest number which can be written in the form of sum of cubes of two numbers in two ways i.e. if $1729 = 9^3 + 10^3 = 1^3 + 12^3$, then the number 1729 is called **Ramanujan's number**.
7. In 1918, Ramanujan and Mr GH Hardy studied the partition function $P(n)$ extensively and gave a non-convergent asymptotic series that permits exact computation of the number of partition of an integer.
8. He discovered mock theta function in last year of his life. For many years, these functions were a mystery but they are now known to be the holomorphic parts of harmonic weak mass forms.

His Publication

1. After his first publication in the 'Journal of the Indian Mathematics society', he gained recognition as genius mathematician with collaboration of English mathematician GH Hardy.
2. He brought forward his **divergent series** that later stimulated research in that given area.
3. He also gave method of analytical number also called as 'Circle method' in Mathematics.

Death

This great mathematician died in 1920. He was one of great mathematician who contributed his life in the field of Mathematics.

Project 3

OBJECTIVE

With rectangle of given perimeter, finding the one with maximum area and rectangle of given area, finding the one with least perimeter.

Prior knowledge

We must be familiar with perimeter and area of geometrical shapes.

Theory

Let l and b be, respectively the length and breadth of the rectangle.

$\therefore$ Perimeter of rectangle $= 2(l + b)$ and Area of rectangle $= l \times b$

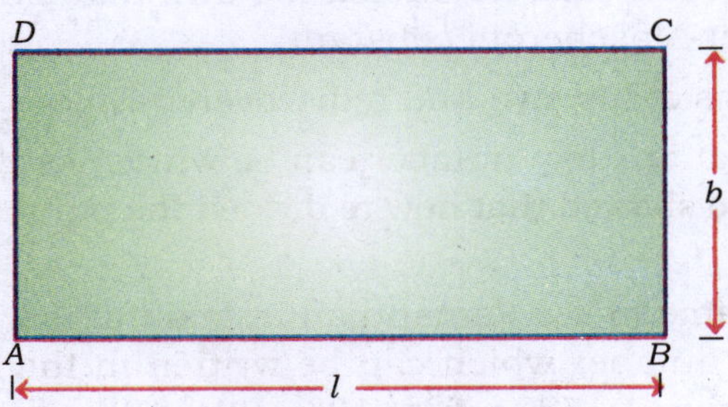

Procedure

1. **Rectangle with Same Perimeters**

   Let us consider the following dimensions of rectangle which results same or equal perimeters but different areas.

S.No.	Length of rectangle (in cm)	Breadth of rectangle (in cm)	Perimeter of rectangle (in cm)	Area of rectangle (in cm^2)
1.	2	6	$2(2+6) = 2 \times 8 = 16$	$2 \times 6 = 12$
2.	3	5	$2(3+5) = 2 \times 8 = 16$	$3 \times 5 = 15$
3.	4	4	$2(4+4) = 2 \times 8 = 16$	$4 \times 4 = 16$ (maximum)
4.	5	3	$2(5+3) = 2 \times 8 = 16$	$5 \times 3 = 15$
5.	6	2	$2(6+2) = 2 \times 8 = 16$	$6 \times 2 = 12$

Here, we see that the area of rectangle is maximum, when the rectangle is a square.

2. **Rectangle with Equal Areas** Let us consider the following dimensions of rectangle which results equal areas but different perimeters.

S. No.	Length of rectangle (in cm)	Breadth of rectangle (in cm)	Area of rectangle (in cm^2)	Perimeter of rectangle (in cm)
1.	1	36	$1 \times 36 = 36$	$2\,(1 + 36) = 2 \times 37 = 74$
2.	2	18	$2 \times 18 = 36$	$2\,(2 + 18) = 2 \times 20 = 40$
3.	3	12	$3 \times 12 = 36$	$2\,(3 + 12) = 2 \times 15 = 30$
4.	4	9	$4 \times 9 = 36$	$2\,(4 + 9) = 2 \times 13 = 26$
5.	6	6	$6 \times 6 = 36$	$2\,(6 + 6) = 2 \times 12 = 24$ (minimum)
6.	9	4	$9 \times 4 = 36$	$2(9 + 4) = 2 \times 13 = 26$
7.	12	3	$12 \times 3 = 36$	$2(12 + 3) = 2 \times 15 = 30$
8.	18	2	$18 \times 2 = 36$	$2(18 + 2) = 2 \times 20 = 40$
9.	36	1	$36 \times 1 = 36$	$2(36 + 1) = 2 \times 37 = 74$

Here, we see that the perimeter of rectangle is minimum when rectangle is square.

Learning Outcomes

From the above tables, we conclude that

1. For all the rectangles with equal perimeters, there exists a square with maximum area.
2. For all the rectangles with equal areas, there exists a square with least (minimum) perimeter.

Project 4

OBJECTIVE

Formula for surface area and volume of solid figures

Prior Knowledge

1. Knowledge of solid figures; right circular cone and sphere.
2. Knowledge of surface area and volume of solid figures.

Theory

1. Solids

The objects which occupy space i.e. they have three dimensions, are called solids.

(i) Surface area of a solid is the area of all of its surface together.

(ii) Volume of a solid is the capacity of solid.

2. Right Circular Cone

A **right circular cone** is a solid generated by revolving a line segment which passes through a fixed point and which makes a constant angle with a fixed line.

(i) O is called the **vertex of the cone**.

(ii) The fixed line OP is called the **axis of the cone**.

(iii) The circle ABC is called the **base of the cone**.

(iv) The length of the line segment joining the vertex O to any point on the circular edge of the base, is called the **slant height of the cone**. Here, $OA = OB$ are the slant heights of the cone.

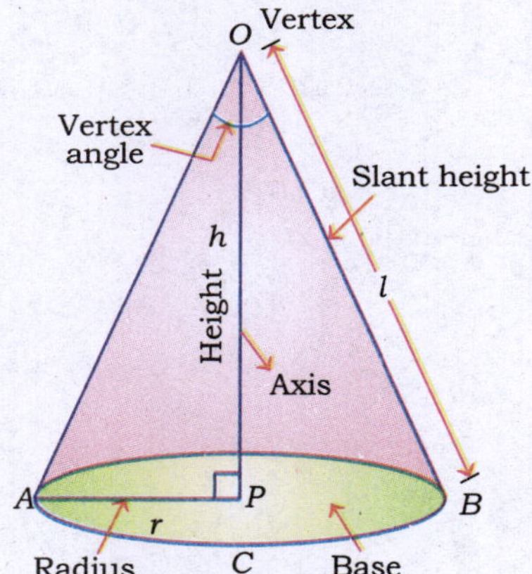

(v) $\angle AOB$ is called the **vertical angle of the cone**.

(vi) The length of the line segment joining the vertex to the centre of the base is called the **height of the cone**. Here, OP is the height of the cone.

(vii) The radius AP of the base circle is called the **radius of the cone**.

(viii) The surface, excluding the base of a right circular cone is called its lateral or curved surface.

3. Sphere

A **sphere** is three dimensional figure (solid figure) which is made up of all points in the space, which lie at a constant distance, from a fixed point called the centre of the sphere and the constant distance is called its radius.

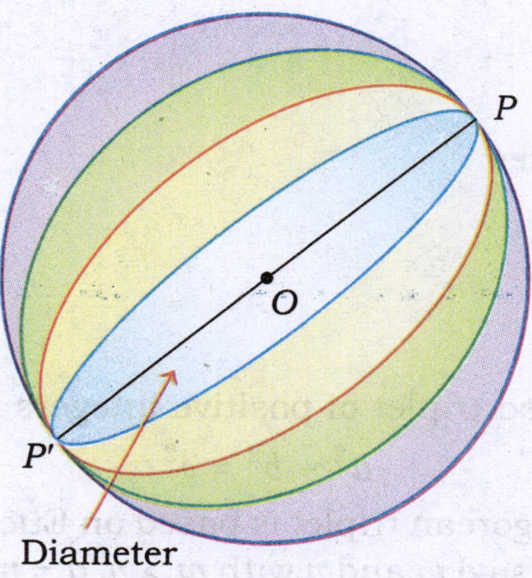

Description

Formulae of the solid figure are given as:

1. Cone

Let height, radius and slant height of a cone be h, r and l, respectively.

(i) Lateral or Curved surface area of cone = πrl sq units

(ii) Total surface area of cone = Curved surface area + Area of base

$= \pi rl + \pi r^2 = \pi r\,(l + r)$ sq units

(iii) Volume of cone = $\frac{1}{3}\pi r^2 h$ cu units

2. Sphere

Let radius of sphere be r. Then,

(i) Surface area of sphere = $4\pi r^2$ sq units

(ii) Volume of sphere = $\frac{4}{3}\pi r^3$ cu units

Learning Outcomes

From the above, we learnt that for various values of dimensions of a solid figure, we can easily determine its required surface area and its volume.

Project 5

OBJECTIVE

Generation of Pythagorean tripletes.

Theory

Introduction

A Pythagorean triplet is an ordered triplet of positive integers (say) a, b and c such that

$$a^2 + b^2 = c^2 \quad \text{...(i)}$$

An effective way to generate Pythagorean triplet is based on Euclid's formula. This formula states that for any two positive integers (say) m and n with $m > n$, $a = m^2 - n^2$, $b = 2\,mn$ and $c = m^2 + n^2$ form a Pythagorean triplet. Though this classical formula generates all primitive triplets (i.e. triplets, which are coprime to each other) but it is incapable of generating all the triplets including non-primitive cases.

e.g. The triplet (15, 36, 39) cannot be generated from the formula rather introducing a multiplier to the triplet (5, 12, 13) does so. We observe that Euclid's formula produces the triplet (5, 12, 13) but does not produce (12, 5, 13). A result of Berggren state that all primitive Pythagorean triplets can be generated using a set of linear transpositions but it requires the triplets to start with (3, 4, 5).

All possible primitive and non-primitive triplets are based on the difference of c and b or c and a which gave only certain distinct values depending on the given number a or b.

Let us consider, $c = b + \Delta$. So, Eq. (i) becomes

$$a^2 + b^2 = (b + \Delta)^2$$

$$\Rightarrow \quad a^2 + b^2 = b^2 + \Delta^2 + 2b\Delta \Rightarrow a^2 = \Delta^2 + 2b\,\Delta \qquad [\because (a+b)^2 = a^2 + b^2 + 2ab]$$

$$\Rightarrow \quad a^2 = \Delta(2b + \Delta) \quad \text{... (ii)}$$

$$\text{or} \quad b = \frac{a^2 - \Delta^2}{2\Delta} \quad \text{... (iii)}$$

Clearly, Eq. (iii) shows that Δ must be a factor of a^2 for the integral values of b.

This is the first condition that prevents Δ possessing any arbitrary value.

Further, we note that b must have positive value i.e. $b > 0$

$$\Rightarrow \quad a^2 - \Delta^2 > 0 \qquad \text{[from Eq. (iii)]}$$

$$\Rightarrow \quad a > \Delta \quad \text{...(iv)}$$

This is called second condition imparted on Δ.

Generating Primitive Pythagorean Triplet

A Pythagorean triplet (a, b, c) is said to be primitive, when a, b, c are coprime to each other i.e. HCF $(a, b, c) = 1$

We know that, c is always odd and only one of a and b is odd, so if we choose a as even, Δ will be even and if we choose a as odd, Δ will be odd.

Description

For Generating Primitive Pythagorean Triplet

1. First, divide the numbers into three categories on the basis of their prime factorisation.
   (i) Even numbers which are only powers of 2.
   (ii) Odd numbers consisting of powers of any prime.
   (iii) Even numbers containing both powers of 2 and other primes.
2. So, we divide our discussion into three subsections.

(i) **Even numbers which are only powers of 2**

Let $a = 2^m$ and $\Delta = 2^r$, where m and r are whole numbers.

Eq.(iv) demands that $m > r$.

Now, from Eq. (ii), we get

$$(2^m)^2 = 2^r\ (2b + 2^r) \Rightarrow b = 2^{r-1}\ (2^{2m-2r} - 1) \qquad \text{...(v)}$$

Since, in this case, a is even, so b must be odd. Now, the right hand side of Eq. (v) will be odd only if $r = 1$.

Hence, the triplet will be $(2^m, 2^{2m-2} - 1, 2^{2m-2} + 1)$.

e.g. Let $\Delta a = 2^4 = 16$

So, $\qquad \Delta = 2$

Hence, $b = 63$ and $c = 65$. Thus, we get (16, 63, 65), which is a primitive triplet.

But if we choose $\Delta \neq 2$, say $\Delta = 8$, we obtain $b = 24$ and $c = 32$. Clearly, the triplet (16, 24, 32) is non-primitive that can be obtained from primitive triplet (2, 3, 4).

So, in this case, the only possible value of Δ is 2.

(ii) **Odd numbers consisting any power of prime number**

Let $a = p^s k$, where p is a prime factor of a and k is the product of other prime factors and s can have any positive integral value.

Then, $\Delta = p^t$, where t is also a whole number.

From Eq. (ii), we get

$$(p^s k)^2 = p^t\ (2b + p^t)$$

$$\Rightarrow \qquad b = \frac{1}{2}(p^{2s-t}\ k^2 - p^t) \qquad \text{...(vi)}$$

Now, for the triplet to be primitive, b must not have p as a factor.

So, from this equation, it is clear that either $t = 0$ or $t = 2s$ provided $a > \Delta$.

Hence, the triplet will be $\left(p^s k, \dfrac{k^2 - p^{2s}}{2}, \dfrac{k^2 + p^{2s}}{2}\right)$, for $\Delta = p^{2s}$

or $\qquad \left(p^s k, \dfrac{p^{2s} k^2 - 1}{2}, \dfrac{p^{2s} k^2 + 1}{2}\right)$, for $\Delta = 1$.

Here, $\Delta = 1$, ensures us that for each odd number, there exists atleast one primitive triplet of the form $\left(a, \dfrac{a^2 - 1}{2}, \dfrac{a^2 + 1}{2}\right)$.

e.g. Let us consider $a = 3^2 \times 11 = 99$. Then, Δ can have two values $\Delta = 3^4 = 81$ or $\Delta = 1$.

For $\Delta = 81$; $b = 20$, $c = 101$. Clearly, (99, 20, 101) forms a primitive triplet.

For $\Delta = 1$; $b = 4900$, $c = 4901$, which again makes a primitive triples (99, 4900, 4901).

In this case, we also observe that if we take $p = 11$, we should have $\Delta = 11^2 = 121$ but it is not possible because it violates Eq. (iv).

(iii) **Even numbers containing both powers of 2 and other primes**

Let $a = 2^m p^s k$, where p is one prime factor of a k is the product of other prime factor and m, s can have any positive integral values.

Then, $\Delta = 2^r p^t$, where r, t are whole numbers.

From Eq. (ii), we get

$$(2^m p^s k)^2 = 2^r p^t (2b + 2^r p^t)$$

$$\Rightarrow \quad b = 2^{r-1} (2^{2m-2r} p^{2s-t} k^2 - p^t) \quad \text{...(vii)}$$

(a) When $m > r$, the terms within the parentheses on right hand side of Eq. (vii) gives odd number, so b will be odd only if $r = 1$. Also p must not be a factor of b for the triplet being primitive that requires $t = 0$ or $t = 2s$.

So, the primitive triplet will be $(2^m p^s k, 2^{2m-2} p^{2s} k^2 - 1, 2^{2m-2} p^{2s} k^2 + 1)$ for $\Delta = 2$

and $(2^m p^s k, 2^{2m-2} k^2 - p^{2s}, 2^{2m-2} k^2 + p^{2s})$ for $\Delta = 2p^{2s}$.

e.g. Let us consider $a = 2^3 5^2 \cdot 27 = 5400$.

Then, Δ can have two values, $\Delta = 2$ and $\Delta = 2 \cdot 5^4 = 1250$.

For $\Delta = 2$; $b = 7289999$, $c = 7290001$

So, the primitive triplet is (5400,7289999, 7290001).

For $\Delta = 1250$; $b = 11039$, $c = 12289$

This gives (5400, 11039, 12289), which is also primitive.

(b) When $m < r$, then Eq. (vii) becomes

$$b = 2^{r-1}\left(\frac{p^{2s-t}k^2}{2^{2r-2m}} - pt\right) = 2^{2m-r-1}(p^{2s-t}k^2 - 2^{2r-2m} p^t) \quad \text{...(viii)}$$

Again the terms within the parentheses on right hand side of Eq. (viii) gives odd number, so b will be odd only if $r = 2m - 1$. Also b should not have p as a factor for the triplet being primitive which requires $t = 0$ or $t = 2s$.

e.g. Let us consider $a = 2^3 3^2 \cdot 49 = 3528$.

Then, Δ will have two values $\Delta = 2^5 = 32$ and $\Delta = 2^5 3^4 = 2592$.

For $\Delta = 32$; $b = 194465$, $c = 194497$

So, we get (3528, 194465, 194497), which is a primitive triplet.

For, $\Delta = 2592$, $b = 1105$, $c = 3697$

This gives (3528, 1105, 3697), which is also primitive.

In this case, if we choose $p = 7$ instead of $p = 3$, it would give $\Delta = 2^5 7^4 = 76832$, which is not permissible, since Δ becomes greater than a.

(c) When $m = r$, then from Eq. (viii),

$$b = 2^{r-1} (p^{2s-t} k^2 - p^t) \quad \text{...(ix)}$$

If $r \geq 1$, b will always be even which gives non-primitive solutions. The only primitive triplets are obtained when $r = m = 0$ but this will lead to Eq. (vi), which we have already discussed.

Here, we noted one of the important point is that when $r = m = 1$, we never obtain a primitive solution so that integers of the configuration $(4n + 2)$ will always give non-primitive triplet.

e.g. The numbers 6, 10, 14, 18, ... will always form non-primitive triplet.

i.e. $6^2 + 8^2 = 10^2$; $10^2 + 24^2 = 26^2$, etc.

If we represent the given number as $a = 2^m\, p_1^{s_1}\, p_2^{s_2} \ldots p_n^{s_n}$, then Δ will be of the form $2^r q$, where $q = p_1^{t_1} p_2^{t_2} \ldots\ldots p_n^{t_n}$ with $t_i = 0$ or $t_i = 2s_i$.

A general example

Let us consider $a = 2^3 \times 3^2 \times 11 = 792$. Here, $p_1 = 3$ and $p_2 = 11$. We show the different cases in the following table.

Primitive triplets for a = 792

Δ	b	(a, b, c)
$2^1\, 3^0\, 11^0 = 2$	156815	(792, 156815, 156817)
$2^1\, 3^4\, 11^0 = 162$	1855	(792, 1855, 2017)
$2^1\, 3^0\, 11^2 = 242$	1175	(792, 1175, 1417)
$2^5\, 3^0\, 11^0 = 32$	9785	(792, 9785, 9817)
$2^5\, 3^4\, 11^0 = 2592$	....	....
$2^5\, 3^0\, 11^2 = 3872$	....	....
$2^1\, 3^4\, 11^2 = 19602$	....	....
$2^5\, 3^4\, 11^2 = 313632$	....	....

Here, the last four values of Δ are not possible because of Eq. (iv). So, only four primitive triplets can be generated for a = 792. Thus, following the previous rules, all possible primitive triplets for a given number can be generated.

For Generating Non-primitive Pythagorean Triplet

In the process of generating non-primitive Pythagorean triplet, the only constraint is $a > \Delta$. So, we first need to factorise the given number and then Δ will be any combination of those factors except the cases for primitive triplets. So, it is obvious that if a is even, Δ must be even and if a is odd, Δ will also be odd.

We illustrate the method by the following example.

Let $a = 60 = 2^2 \times 3 \times 5$. Again, we show various cases in the following table.

Non-primitive triplets for a = 60

Δ	b	(a, b, c)
$2^2 3^0 5^0 = 4$	448	(60, 448, 452)
$2^1 3^1 5^0 = 6$	297	(60, 297, 303)
$2^1 3^0 5^1 = 10$	175	(60, 175, 185)
$2^2 3^1 5^0 = 12$	144	(60, 144, 156)
$2^2 3^0 5^1 = 20$	80	(60, 80, 100)
$2^3 3^1 5^0 = 24$	63	(60, 63, 87)
$2^1 3^1 5^1 = 30$	45	(60, 45, 75)
$2^2 3^2 5^0 = 36$	32	(60, 32, 68)
$2^3 3^0 5^1 = 40$	25	(60, 25, 65)

Here, Δ = 2, 8, 18 and 50 have not been taken because they generate primitive triplets and the other combinations of the factors have been discarded as they violate Eq. (iv).

Thus, finding all the possible values of Δ, we can obtain all non-primitive triplets.

Project 6

OBJECTIVE

Making odd numbered

Prior knowledge

We must know the magic square.

Material Required

Drawing sheet and geometry box.

Theory

Magic Square

In recreational Mathematics, a magic square is an arrangement of different integers in a square grid, where the sum of numbers in each row, in each column is equal to the sum of numbers in each diagonal . A magic square always have the same number of rows and columns.

Let n be the number of rows, then the number of columns is also n. Thus, the magic square always contains $n \times n$, (n^2) numbers and its size is described as being 'of order n'. A magic square that contains the integers from 1 to n^2, is called a normal magic square. Normal magic squares of all sizes except $n = 2$ can be constructed, although the case $n = 1$ is a trivial case, consisting of a single cell containing the number 1.

The smallest non-trivial case, 3 × 3 is shown below.

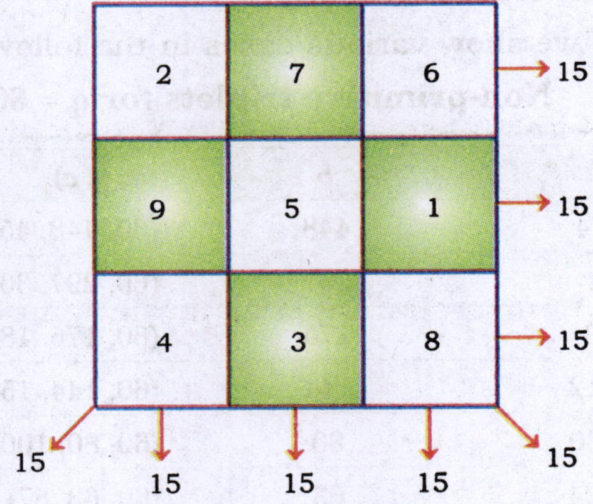

Procedure

1. Draw a pyramid on each side of the magic square as given below.

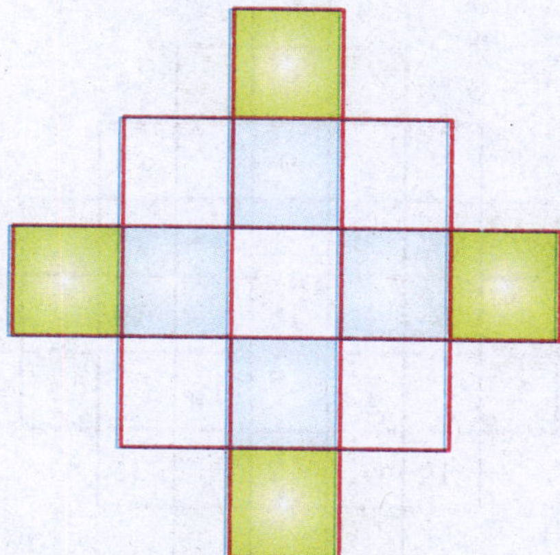

2. The pyramid should have two less squares on its base than the number of squares on the side of the magic square.
3. Sequentially place the numbers 1 to n^2 in the diagonals as shown in the given figure.

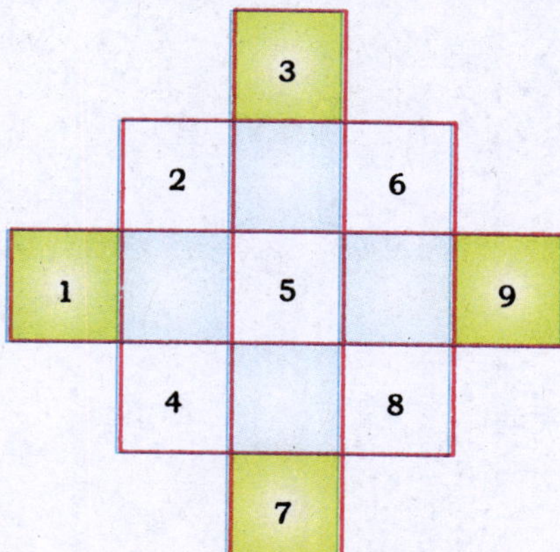

4. Relocate the numbers not in $n \times n$ square (that appears in the pyramids you added) to the opposite blank space inside the square.

Result

From the above procedure, we have got the following magic square.

2	7	6
9	5	1
4	3	8

Do Yourself

Follow the above procedure and complete the following magic square.

3		9		15
	8		14	
7		13		19
	12		18	
11		17		23

Project 7

OBJECTIVE

Application of Algebra in day-to-day life.

Prior Knowledge

We must be familiar with basic concepts of algebra and concept of pair of linear equations.

Theory

An algebric equation of the form $ax + by + c = 0$, where a, b and c are the real numbers ($a \neq 0$, $b \neq 0$), is **called linear equations in two variables** (say) x and y.

Example

Let us take an example from day-to-day life. Harsh and Madhu, each has a certain number of mangoes. Harsh says to Madhu," if you give 30 of your mangoes, I will have twice as many as left with you." Madhu replies "if you give the 10, I will have thrice as many as left with you." How many mangoes do they have together?

Procedure

1. Consider suitable variables for the given statement. Let number of mangoes Harsh has = x and number of mangoes Madhu has = y
2. Write down two equations, one equation must be related to first condition and other equation must be related to second condition.

   Equation representing first condition is given as

   $$(x + 30) = 2(y - 30)$$
   $$\Rightarrow \quad x + 30 = 2y - 60$$
   $$\Rightarrow \quad x - 2y + 90 = 0$$

   Equation representing second condition is given as

   $$3(x - 10) = (y + 10)$$
   $$\Rightarrow \quad 3x - 30 = y + 10 \Rightarrow 3x - y - 40 = 0$$
3. Now, solve the above equations by any method that you have already studied in your class.

Actual calculation

Let us solve the following equations by substitution method, we get

$$x - 2y + 90 = 0 \quad \text{...(i)}$$
$$3x - y - 40 = 0 \quad \text{...(ii)}$$

From Eq. (ii) $\quad y = 3x - 40$

On substituting $y = 3x - 40$ in Eq. (i), we get $x - 2(3x - 40) + 90 = 0$

$\therefore \quad x =$ ....

Now, on substituting $x =$ .... in $y = 3x - 40$, we get $y =$ ....

Thus, together they have .... number of mangoes

Experiment/Activity No.________ Date ________ Page No. ________

Teacher Signature________________

Experiment/Activity No.________ Date ________ Page No. ________

Teacher Signature ________________

Experiment/Activity No.________ Date ________ Page No. ________

Teacher Signature ________________

Experiment/Activity No.________ Date ________ Page No. ________

Teacher Signature________________

Experiment/Activity No.________ Date ________ Page No. ________

Teacher Signature ________________

Experiment/Activity No.________ Date ________ Page No. ________

Teacher Signature ________

Experiment/Activity No.________ Date ________ Page No. ________

Teacher Signature ________________

Experiment/Activity No.________ Date ________ Page No. ________

Teacher Signature ________

Experiment/Activity No.________ Date ________ Page No. ________

Teacher Signature ____________

Experiment/Activity No.________ Date ________ Page No. ________

Teacher Signature ________

Experiment/Activity No.________ Date ________ Page No. ________

Teacher Signature ________________

Experiment/Activity No.________ Date ________ Page No. ________

Teacher Signature ________

Experiment/Activity No.________ Date ________ Page No. ________

Teacher Signature ________

Experiment/Activity No.________ Date ________ Page No. ________

Teacher Signature ________

Experiment/Activity No.________ Date ________ Page No. ________

Teacher Signature ________

Experiment/Activity No.________ Date ________ Page No. ________

Teacher Signature ________

Experiment/Activity No.________ Date ________ Page No. ________

Teacher Signature ________

Experiment/Activity No.________ Date ________ Page No. ________

Teacher Signature ________________

Experiment/Activity No.________ Date ________ Page No. ________

Teacher Signature ________________

Experiment/Activity No.________ Date ________ Page No. ________

Teacher Signature ________________

Experiment/Activity No.________ Date ________ Page No. ________

Teacher Signature ________________

Experiment/Activity No.________ Date ________ Page No. ________

Teacher Signature ______________

Experiment/Activity No.________ Date ________ Page No. ________

Teacher Signature ____________________

Experiment/Activity No.________ Date ________ Page No. ________

Teacher Signature ____________

Experiment/Activity No.________ Date ________ Page No. ________

Teacher Signature ________________

Experiment/Activity No.________ Date ________ Page No. ________

Teacher Signature____________

Experiment/Activity No.________ Date ________ Page No. ________

Teacher Signature ________________

Experiment/Activity No.________ Date ________ Page No. ________

Teacher Signature ________

Experiment/Activity No.________ Date ________ Page No. ________

Teacher Signature ________

Experiment/Activity No.________ Date ________ Page No. ________

Teacher Signature ________________

Experiment/Activity No.________ Date ________ Page No. ________

Teacher Signature ________

Experiment/Activity No.________ Date ________ Page No. ________

Teacher Signature ________________

Experiment/Activity No.________ Date ________ Page No. ________

Teacher Signature ________________

Experiment/Activity No.________ Date ________ Page No. ________

Teacher Signature ________________

Experiment/Activity No.________ Date ________ Page No. ________

Teacher Signature________________

Experiment/Activity No.________ Date ________ Page No. ________

Teacher Signature ______________

Experiment/Activity No.________ Date ________ Page No. ________

Teacher Signature________________

Experiment/Activity No.________ Date ________ Page No. ________

Teacher Signature ________________

Experiment/Activity No.________ Date ________ Page No. ________

Teacher Signature ________________

Experiment/Activity No.________ Date ________ Page No. ________

Teacher Signature ________________

Experiment/Activity No.________ Date ________ Page No. ________

Teacher Signature ________________

Experiment/Activity No.________ Date ________ Page No. ________

Teacher Signature ________

Experiment/Activity No.________ Date ________ Page No. ________

Teacher Signature ________________

Experiment/Activity No.________ Date ________ Page No. ________

Teacher Signature ________

Experiment/Activity No.________ Date ________ Page No. ________

Teacher Signature ________

Experiment/Activity No.________ Date ________ Page No. ________

Teacher Signature ________________

Experiment/Activity No.________ Date ________ Page No. ________

Teacher Signature ____________

Experiment/Activity No.________ Date ________ Page No. ________

Teacher Signature ________

Experiment/Activity No.________ Date ________ Page No. ________

Teacher Signature ________

Experiment/Activity No.________ Date ________ Page No. ________

Teacher Signature ________

Experiment/Activity No.________ Date ________ Page No. ________

Teacher Signature ________________

Experiment/Activity No.________ Date ________ Page No. ________

Teacher Signature ________________

Experiment/Activity No.________ Date ________ Page No. ________

Teacher Signature ________________

Experiment/Activity No.________ Date ________ Page No. ________

Teacher Signature ____________________

Experiment/Activity No.________ Date ________ Page No. ________

Teacher Signature ________________

Experiment/Activity No.________ Date ________ Page No. ________

Teacher Signature ________________

Experiment/Activity No.________ Date ________ Page No. ________

Teacher Signature ________

Experiment/Activity No.________ Date ________ Page No. ________

Teacher Signature ________________

Experiment/Activity No.________ Date ________ Page No. ________

Teacher Signature ________________

Experiment/Activity No.________ Date ________ Page No. ________

Teacher Signature ________

Experiment/Activity No.________ Date ________ Page No. ________

Teacher Signature ________________

Experiment/Activity No.________ Date ________ Page No. ________

Teacher Signature ____________

Experiment/Activity No.________ Date ________ Page No. ________

Teacher Signature ________

Experiment/Activity No.________ Date ________ Page No. ________

Teacher Signature ________